Landmark Visitors Guide

North Devon & Exmoor

Richard Sale & Brian Le Messurier

Published by
Landmark Publishing
Ashbourne Hall, Cokayne Ave, Ashbourne,
Derbyshire DE6 1EJ England

Landmark Visitors Guide

North Devon
& Exmoor

Richard Sale & Brian Le Messurier

Contents

Contents

Introduction

Virtually every area of England claims to be the most beautiful, the most historic, the most *English* of them all. For each, in its own way, this is doubtless correct, but for many who flock to the South-West each year it is the counties of Devon and Somerset that represent idyllic England – a land of glorious scenery and quaint countryfolk. Somerset has its cider orchards and a host of country pubs each filled with locals in smocks drinking scrumpy; Devon its beaches and cream teas. For the tourist these generalisations can seem true – and the tourist industry regularly goes out of its way to prove them true – but the visitor who gets behind the mask will find much

more. Somerset and Devon share Exmoor which, though upland moor, is a lower, more user-friendly place than its southern neighbour Dartmoor. To the north, Exmoor drops into the sea along a coast of great beauty. Although more sheltered than the North Devon coast, the rugged cliffs near Ilfracombe and Baggy Point are the equal of anything on the county's southern coast, or even Cornwall. As well as being scenically splendid, the area is historically fascinating, virtually every village having a tale to tell. And this is the land of *Lorna Doone*, surely the most romantic of all English novels.

This book explores all aspects of the area, its history and natural history, its myth and legend. It also details all the places the visitor can go – to learn more about the area, to enjoy its arts and crafts, its parks and gardens, or just to be entertained; this is, after all, one of the prime holiday areas of England.

Exmoor is naturally divided into two, the Exe/Quarme and Avill valleys, followed by the A396, dividing the Brendon Hills from the main mass of Exmoor. We explore the Brendon Hills in Chapter 1. The main moor is arbitrarily divided into two by the B3223/B3358 roads that cross the central moor. That part of

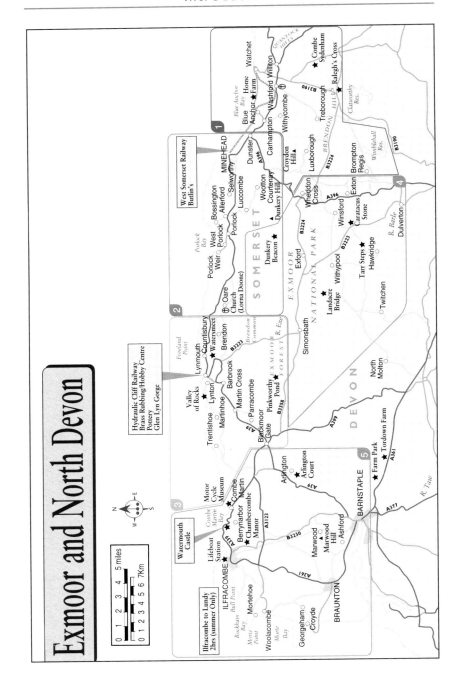

Exmoor and North Devon

the National Park which lies to the north of the divide can itself be divided into two convenient regions, Somerset's Exmoor to the west and Devon's Exmoor to the east. These two areas, which meet at County Gate, are explored in Chapters 2 and 3. Chapter 4 deals with the southern section of the moor, while Chapter 5 explores north Devon, that part of the county which lies to the west of Exmoor.

A SHORT HISTORY

It is not clear whether Exmoor was ever glaciated. Although never covered with an ice sheet, the Punchbowl near Winsford looks very similar to glacial corries. But even if it was not ice covered, the moor was frozen at times and unlikely to have been permanently inhabited. It is likely that man moved in soon after, flint tools dating from the Mesolithic (Middle Stone) Age having been found which probably date from as early as 8,000BC. From that time man's occupation of the moor has been continuous, though it was several thousand years before he left a permanent reminder of his presence on the landscape.

No Neolithic long barrows exist on today's moor, though there is evidence at some sites of a Neolithic presence. The first definite moorland dwellers arrived with the Bronze Age, the moor being dotted with round barrows, the distinctive burial mounds of Bronze Age folk, and with their megalithic sites. The word megalith simply means 'big stone'. Circles, rows and standing stones are among the moor's most enigmatic features, often set in remote landscapes where their mystery is enhanced.

The moor also shows signs of occupation by the next great cultural wave to have swept in from mainland Europe – the iron-using Celts. The Celts built forts into which they could retreat when threatened, choosing hill tops which they reinforced with ditches and ramparts. Several of these can be seen on the moor and in north Devon. Beyond the moor the Celts were eventually absorbed into the Roman empire, but soon re-established their tribal way of life after the Roman departure. These tribal conflicts allowed the Saxons to conquer England. In the South-West the Saxons pushed the Celts back into Cornwall. But by then the climate, which had allowed Bronze Age man to settle the moor, had changed and the Exmoor plateau was a harsh environment for settlers.

Viking raids on the coast – there are recorded raids on Watchet and Porlock – meant that the Saxons had to be on their guard. It was during this period of tension that the settlement of the moorland fringes was established much as it is now. The upland was still largely untamed, and remained so when the Normans came, the moor being turned into a Royal Forest. The word 'forest' here is misleading in its modern context, the forests of Norman England being hunting preserves which could include upland moor and heath as well as real woodland. As a forest Exmoor was subject to its own forest laws, which protected the wildlife, specifically the deer, and forbade the damaging of trees, the grazing of animals etc. These laws were strictly enforced and the punishment for transgressors was savage.

The Royal Forest of Exmoor ended when the Civil War resulted in the ousting of the king. When

Parliament disposed of the Forest it was bought by James Boevey, a man of Dutch ancestry, an intellectual who spoke eight languages, but a man much given to making enemies and of fighting them in court. Boevey began the process of creating the moor we see today both as owner and, after the property was restored to the monarchy, as tenant. He was helped in this by later tenants, including the Aclands who revived stag hunting and so amalgamated the medieval and modern aspects of the moor and the Knights, who bought much of the area from the Crown and attempted to improve it for agriculture.

THE EXMOOR NATIONAL PARK

Exmoor's beauty and importance was recognised by the granting of National Park status in the 1950s. Of all the National Parks in England and Wales, Exmoor has the greatest range of natural scenery. While it has none of the rugged grandeur of the mountains of Snowdonia or the Lake District, or the bleak upland moors of Dartmoor or such an extent or range of sea cliff as the Pembrokeshire Coastal park, Exmoor has a little of all of them and a bit more besides.

The Park's upland is divided into two sections by the River Exe, which gives the moor its name, and by its tributary, the Quarme, with the Brendon Hills (not to be confused with Brendon Common, which lies in Doone country to the west) to the east and the main Exmoor plateau to the west. On its north-eastern edge Exmoor falls into gentle, wooded country studded with beautiful villages such as Selworthy and Dunster.

Underlying Exmoor are rocks of the Devonian period, sandstones and grits. These hard, resistant rocks yield a poor, acidic soil that supports a very limited vegetation. On the Devonian slates and shales the soil is a little better and it supports a greater range and growth of vegetation, making the river valleys more sheltered to give a better growing environment, greener and more lush, a real delight to the eye. In the valleys oaks are the predominant tree, but there are also stands of beech and ash as well as other, less numerous, species.

WILDLIFE OF THE MOOR

On the high moor the vegetation is chiefly grasses and sedges and, on surrounding commons, heather – ling and bell heather – with clumps of bilberry (known locally as whortleberry). The former offers a glorious purple show when it blossoms.

On the high moor the animal life is limited: a few Exmoor ponies and, but rarely, deer. The latter, the native red deer together with roe and introduced herds of fallow, are mainly encountered in the wooded valleys. Moorland birds are not abundant, despite the fact that over 200 species have been noted within the Park's boundaries, but the buzzard is frequently seen, working the thermals of the up-slopes as it searches for a meal. Bird-watchers will choose the wooded valleys rather than the moor if they are after variety, and will doubtless travel north to the coast to complete their survey, for there, with the moor still visible behind them, razorbills can be added to a list that may also include stonechat, dipper and kingfisher.

Watchet Museum

To the east of Dunkery Beacon lie the Brendon Hills, the eastern part of the Exmoor National Park, a section of the Park too often overlooked by visitors.

NEARBY COAST

The Quantocks, Britain's smallest Area of Outstanding Natural Beauty, stand clear of the Somerset plain, a well-defined upland that beckons the visitor. To the west, Watchet is a famous port, but when the visitor is hurrying towards high Exmoor and the delightful villages of Dunster, Selworthy, Porlock, too often the gentle landscape of the Brendon Hills is missed. In this chapter we explore that delightful landscape.

The visitor heading to Exmoor by taking the A39 westwards from the M5 motorway soon reaches **Williton,** a small town that in medieval times was the main village of the local area. That importance, reinforced by the building of a turnpike road in the early nineteenth century, accounts for the present-day size. There is a long history of markets and fairs, and the hospital, on the western side of the town, is housed in the Union Workhouse, built in the 1830s. On the opposite side of the town is a station of the West Somerset Railway (see Minehead).

To the south-east of the town is Orchard Mill, probably dating from the early seventeenth century, though the present mill, powered by an over-shot waterwheel, dates from the nineteenth century. The mill is now home to the **Bakelite Museum** with a collection which explores the fascinating history of plastics from Victorian times (when substances as varied as egg-white, crushed beetles, pigs' blood and soot were used to create mouldable materials) to more modern materials. There is a children's play area and a very good café (home-made clotted cream teas a speciality). Closer to the centre of town the **Williton Pottery** exhibits the hand-made work of Martin Pettinger. The Pottery has both a

Williton and Thomas à Becket

After the Norman Conquest Williton was 'owned' by the Conqueror himself, but eventually passed to his grand-daughter Maud and her husband Richard Fitzurse. The couple owned several properties, but their son Reginald lived at Williton. Reginald Fitzurse was one of the four knights who murdered Thomas à Becket in Canterbury Cathedral. Legend has it that Fitzurse was the leader of the four knights and that it was he who actually struck the first blow. After the killing, Reginald, together with two of the other three murderers, returned to Williton. After that their story is as much legend as fact. They seem to have gone to Scotland, then to Rome from where the Pope banished them to the Holy Land. One version of the story has Reginald eventually settling in Ireland. What seems to be true is that he gave half his estate to the Knights Templar, almost certainly as an act of contrition for his part in the murder, and the other half to his brother who built a chapel at Williton where men could pray for Becket and his brother's soul. Nothing of this remains. Another of the four murderers was Richard de Brett (or Brito) from the village of Sampford Brett, a short distance to the south-east of Williton.

shop and an exhibition gallery.

From Williton a road heads north to Watchet, passing ancient earthworks known locally as Battle Gore, reputedly the site of a battle between Saxons and Vikings in the tenth century. **Watchet** is a lovely little port and town, justifiably popular with visitors. It has been popular ever since seaside holidays became the vogue.

The Rime of the Ancient Mariner

Samuel Taylor Coleridge is said to have been enchanted with Watchet: it is widely believed among experts that *The Rime of the Ancient Mariner* was begun in the Bell Inn in Market Street and that the mariner's journey began from Watchet where the port does indeed sit 'below the kirk, below the hill, below the light house top'.

The town is set at a natural break in the coastal cliffs and was obviously of importance as a port in Saxon times as a royal mint was set up here. Some of the minted coins can be seen in the town museum. Interestingly, others can be seen in museums in Scandinavia, having found their way there as booty from Viking raids or, perhaps, as *danegeld*, the 'protection money' paid to the Vikings to avoid raids.

The **town museum**, housed in the old Market House in Market Street, close to the port, also has fossils excavated from the local cliffs and a collection based on the Brendon Hills' iron ore mines and the railway which brought the ore to the port. The railway followed the Washford River to the port, the shipment of ore to South Wales making Watchet a very prosperous place in the mid-nineteenth century. The line was later incorporated into what is now the West Somerset Railway, which has a station in the town. Alabaster, hewn from the local cliffs and made into funerary monuments and effigies, added to the port's prosperity.

Opposite the Station the Boat Museum explores the history of the flatner, a double-ended boat with no keel, which was once used all over Somerset.

Watchet's church, a fine building dating mainly from the sixteenth century, lies away from the port, to the south-west. The church has several good monuments to the Wyndham family.

ST DECUMAN

Watchet's church is dedicated to St Decuman, a sixth-century Welshman who is said to have crossed the Bristol Channel – legend has it on his cloak as a raft, or perhaps on a sheep hurdle – accompanied only by a cow whose milk he drank. He is said to have landed at Watchet and set up a hermitage on the closest hill. One day he was murdered by local thieves who cut off his head. In typical fashion his body is said to have picked up the head, washed it in a local well and then re-crossed the Channel with the head tucked under his arm. Later the church was built close to Decuman's hermit site and the well.

THE LIVE CORPSE

Soon after her marriage to John Wyndham, whose father had inherited the lordship of Watchet in the mid-sixteenth century, Florence

13

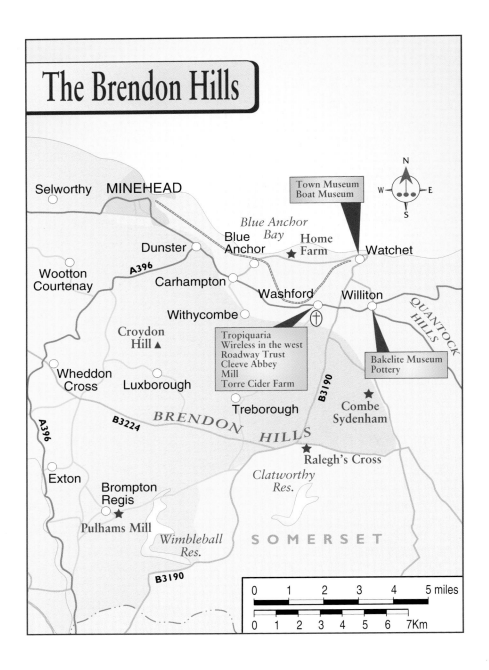

The Brendon Hills

Selworthy · MINEHEAD

Blue Anchor Bay

Blue Anchor · Home Farm · Watchet

Town Museum
Boat Museum

N
W E
S

Dunster

A396

Wootton
Courtenay

Carhampton

Washford · Williton

Withycombe

QUANTOCK HILLS

Croydon
Hill ▲

Tropiquaria
Wireless in the west
Roadway Trust
Cleeve Abbey
Mill
Torre Cider Farm

Bakelite Museum
Pottery

Wheddon
Cross

Luxborough

B3190

Treborough

Combe
Sydenham

A396

B3224

BRENDON

HILLS

Ralegh's Cross

Exton

Brompton
Regis

*Clatworthy
Res.*

Pulhams Mill

*Wimbleball
Res.*

SOMERSET

B3190

0	1	2	3	4	5 miles

0	1	2	3	4	5	6	7Km

Above: Bakelite Museum, Orchard Mill, Williton

Below: Cleeve Abbey, where many of the buildings are intact

Wadham died suddenly. Her body was taken to the Wyndham family vault in Watchet church. After it had been laid out the sexton, left alone with the corpse, decided to steal the expensive rings left on her wedding finger. These proved impossible to pull off, so he took a knife to the finger. At the first cut Florence promptly sat up, fully conscious and revived. Florence lived a full life, though whether the sexton survived the experience, or what happened to him, is not recorded.

West of Williton, along the A39, lies **Washford**, a pleasant village close to several interesting visitor sites. To the east, towards Williton, the near Washford Cross (and the radio masts) **Tropiquaria** has a collection of small animals and birds, lizards and spiders, some of which can be handled. There is also an aquarium. The site has a café and a picnic room, and a puppet theatre. The site is housed in an old BBC transmission building and so it is appropriate that it is also home to **Wireless in the West**, a history of radio broadcasting with a collection of old transmission equipment and wirelesses.

Closer to the village, the station on the old **Somerset and Dorset Railway** – the West Somerset Railway runs on the adjacent line – is a museum of the old line. The museum has a huge collection of memorabilia and a reconstructed signal box. To the south of the village is **Cleeve Abbey**, the most complete monastic house in Somerset. The abbey was founded, in the beautifully named *Vallis Florida*, the Valley of Flowers, in the 1180s for Cistercian monks. The thirteenth-century gatehouse remains, as do many of the abbey's domestic build-

ings, set around the cloisters. The chamber near the Chapter House retains a medieval wall painting, while the fifteenth-century refectory has a magnificent timber roof with carved angels.

To the south of the village **Washford Mill** has been converted into a shop where locally made produce, arts and crafts are exhibited and sold. Further south, the **Torre Cider Farm** offers visitors the chance to sample ciders straight from the barrel as well as having a display of old cider presses, a farm shop (selling locally made cheeses) and farm animals to thrill younger visitors. The farm also has a studio making silk flowers and embroidery, and scented candles.

To the north of Washford, in the churchyard of **Old Cleeve**, the grave of George Jones, the village blacksmith in the late eighteenth century, is marked with the famous blacksmith's epitaph.

THE BLACKSMITH'S EPITAPH

My sledge and hammer lie reclined
My bellows too have lost their wind
My fire's extinct, my forge decayed
And in the dust my body's laid
My coal is burnt, my iron's gone
My nails are drove, my work is done

To the west of Washford is **Carhampton**, a large village reputedly founded by the Celtic St Carantoc. He sailed across the Bristol Channel from South Wales on a large stone altar, which he set up in a church he built on land given to him by King Arthur after he had disposed of a fiery dragon which was plaguing the locals. Carhampton is one of the few villages in Somerset where the ancient tradition of wassailing the apple orchards to ensure a good crop is still performed on Twelfth Night. To the south of Carhampton, nestling at the foot of the Brendon Hills and just inside the Exmoor National Park, is **Withycombe**, a pretty village with an interesting church. In it are two very early (late thirteenth- or early fourteenth-century) effigies holding hearts, probably representing heart burials from the period when a local lord might own several properties and have his body distributed for burial in the church at each. There is also a brass to Joan Carne.

The Withycombe Witch

Joan Carne, who lived at Sandhill on the eastern edge of Withycombe, in the time of Shakespeare, is said to have been a witch who murdered, or cast spells to cause of the death of, all three of her husbands. Despite this Joan seems to have been reasonably well liked by her neighbours for many attended her funeral. However, when they gathered back at her house after the service they found Joan's ghost preparing a meal of bacon and eggs for them.

To the north of Carhampton is the small holiday resort of **Blue Anchor**, named for a seventeenth-century inn. To the east of Blue Anchor are crumbling alabaster cliffs on which stood a chapel, built in the fifteenth century. It housed a statue of Our Lady of the Sea to which pilgrimages were made, until a section of cliff collapsed, dumping the build-ing into the sea. The road eastwards from Blue Anchor follows the shore line, passing **Home Farm** where visitors can make friends with the animals and enjoy the home-made cakes or home-produced ham.

THE EASTERN BRENDON HILLS

Heading south from Washford, through Torre, the visitor enters the Exmoor National Park, soon reaching Fair Cross at the Park boundary. From here, follow the B3188 to **Monksilver**, where, in the church on 18 June 1583, Sir Francis Drake married Elizabeth Sydenham. The village, named for the sparkling waters of the stream that runs through it and for its one-time possession by the monks of Goldcliff Priory in Monmouthshire (the Lord of the Manor, Robert de Chandos had endowed the priory), has some lovely thatched cottages.

Further along the main road is the **Combe Sydenham Country Park**, centred on the fine Elizabethan manor house built by Sir George Sydenham. The house can be toured: one of the items on display is the cannonball supposedly fired from the other side of the world by Sir Francis Drake to (successfully) cause the abandonment of Elizabeth Sydenham's wedding to a local man so that Drake could marry her on his return. The country park beside the house has several miles of waymarked trails, as well as testing trails for mountain bikers (bikes can be hired) and 4x4 drive vehicles.

South of Combe Sydenham the B3188 passes the village of **Elworthy** – the church here is mostly thirteenth- century. One rector was John

Selleck; driven from office after the Civil War because of his staunch Royalist views, he helped the future Charles II escape. Turn right at Elworthy Cross and follow the B3224 up on to the Brendon Hills. The name 'brendon' means 'brown hills' and, possibly, is different in origin to the village of Brendon on Brendon Common. The latter, on the west side of Exmoor, near Doone Country, derives from 'broom', the plant.

There is little moorland now on the Brendons, but there are still wonderful views as the road rises to **Ralegh's Cross**. The origin of the name is uncertain, but most likely from a member of the de Ralegh family, a fourteenth-century knight killed in the wars against the French, whose body was rested here on its way to his Nettlecombe estate. Further west the ridge top road forks: to the left the B3190 passes Beverton Pond, the source of the River Tone which flows through Taunton, then ascends Haddon Hill (see below). On the B3224, just beyond Sea View House, to the right, are the remains of an incline built down the hillside to transport iron ore towards the coast. The incline can be viewed by following the marked footpath that leaves the main road: there is also a fine waterfall close to the incline. The old railway, which ran to the top of the incline, lies to the left of the road, and the remains of the engine house can still be seen.

THE NAKED BOY'S STONE

The boundary stone lies on the southern side of the B3224 marking the point where four local parishes meet. The name derives from a curious legend that during the Beating of the Bounds, carried out at regular intervals many years ago, a naked boy was required to stand on, or walk around, the stone. On an early nineteenth-century map the stone is marked as Four Naked Boys, implying that a 'volunteer' from each parish performed the (in view of the exposed nature of the site), somewhat chilling ritual. Another legend claims the stone is a petrified drunken man and that at midnight each night it/he walks down the hill to quench his raging thirst.

THE WESTERN BRENDON HILLS

To the north of the B3224 there are now heavily wooded, folded hills. Tucked into the folds are 'secret' villages – **Luxborough**, where the Royal Oak is a popular country inn, and **Treborough**, once famous for its iron mines and slate quarry: the slates for Dunster Castle came from here. To the south is **Withiel Florey** where the neat church – the tower is thirteenth century – hides behind a farm. Also southwards is **Wimbleball Lake**, a reservoir created in 1980 that is now also a water park with sailing, rowing and fishing, shoreline nature trails and a café. The lake, which covers almost 400 acres (about150 hectares) and holds about 4,000 million gallons (around 20,000 million litres) of water, has a flourishing population of water birds. Close to the western shore is **Brompton Regis**. The 'king' (*regis*) of Brompton Regis was William the Conqueror who took the estate himself as it had been held by Gytha, King Harold's mother.

Close to Brompton Regis, Pulhams Mill, one of Exmoor's

Above: Watchet Station Below: Washford Railway Museum

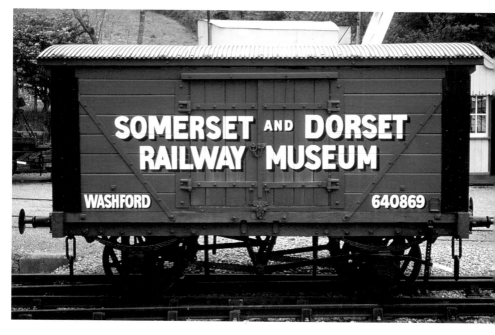

oldest mill sites, is now a craft centre and tea rooms.

To the south of Wimbleball Lake lies **Haddon Hill**. From the car park close to its summit the top is easily reached: it is a marvellous viewpoint. To the north, below the hill, there is a superb riverside walk through Hartford Bottom, the wooded valley of the River Haddeo. The river can be followed all the way to **Bury**, where it can be crossed by ford or over a delightful packhorse bridge.

THE BELL OF BARLYNCH PRIORY

From Bury a narrow road climbs steep Bury Hill, with excellent views west over Barlynch Wood and Farm. The farm incorporates stone from the twelfth century Barlynch Priory. The house was never rich and finally closed in the fifteenth century. The bell from the church was taken to Exeter where, it is claimed by loyal Somerset men, its first tolling turned all the Devon cream in the city sour. The name 'barlynch' means barley hill from the crop once grown on its flanks.

North of Bury the A396, which follows the western border of the Brendon Hills, is set close to the Exe, and then to its tributary the Quarme, as it climbs to Wheddon Cross. To the east of the road are three final Brendon villages. **Exton** is a straggling, but pretty, place with an ancient church, while **Cutcombe**, close to Wheddon Cross, is well-positioned for the walker between Dunkery Beacon and Lype Hill, the highest point of the Brendon Hills. A strong walker could complete a walk which takes in both, but most will content themselves with a walk which visits Lype Hill's summit (at 1388ft – 423m), returning along the western flank of Kersham Hill.

Beyond the turn to Cutcombe the A396 drops down Cutcombe Hill as it heads for the coast. Further on is the turn for **Timberscombe**, named for its position in a wooded valley between Exmoor and the Brendon Hills. In the 1950s a rare sixteenth-century mural was uncovered on the wall of the church here, one of the few to have survived the Puritan purges. Visitors who venture to the Brendons in late winter/early spring should ask the way to Snowdrop Valley, famous for its displays at that time.

Beyond Timberscombe the main road descends to Dunster, starting point for our exploration of high Exmoor.

Places to Visit

Brendon Hills

Bakelite Museum

Orchard Mill, Williton
Open: Easter-September Thursday-Sunday 10.30am-6pm (open daily in school holidays).
☎ 01984 632133

Williton Pottery

Half Acre, Williton
Open: All year, Monday-Saturday 10am-5pm
(closes at 1pm on Saturdays)
☎ 01984 632150

Watchet Museum

Market Street
Open: April-October, daily 10.30am-4.30pm. ☎ 01984 631345

Watchet Boat Museum

Harbour Road
Open: Easter-October, Tuesday – Thursday, Saturday and Sunday 2-4pm
☎ 01984 633117/634242

Tropiquaria/Wireless in the West

Washford Cross
Open: Easter-mid-September, daily 10am-6pm; mid-September-October, daily 11am-5pm; November, February and March, Saturday, Sunday and school holidays 11am-dusk.
☎ 01984 640688

Somerset and Dorset Railway Museum

Washford Station
Open: March-October, 10am-5pm.
☎ 01984 640869

Cleeve Abbey (English Heritage)

Washford
Open: April-October, daily 10am-6pm or dusk
☎ 01984 640377

Washford Mill

Washford
Open: All year, Monday-Saturday 9am-5pm, Sunday and Bank Holidays 10am-4pm
☎ 01984 640412

Torre Cider Farm and Silk Orchard

Torre, Washford
Open: March-October, daily 9am-6pm; November-February, daily 10am-4pm.
☎ 01984 640004

Home Farm

Blue Anchor
Open: Easter-October, daily 10.30am-5.30pm.
☎ 01984 640817

Combe Sydenham Country Park

Open: Park: April-September, daily 9am-4.30pm
House: Guided tours by appointment
☎ 0800 7838572

Pulhams Mill

Brompton Regis
Open: All year Monday-Saturday 10am-5pm, Sunday 12.30-5pm
☎ 01398 371366

2. Somerset's Exmoor

T hat part of Exmoor which lies in Somerset includes Dunkery Beacon, the highest peak on the moor. It also includes Dunster and Porlock, two of the most famous of Exmoor's villages and overlooks a fine section of coast.

DUNSTER

Dunster has a claim to being not only one of the finest villages in Somerset, but also in England. It is a beautiful place, almost every building having an enviable history, and the whole being exquisitely positioned below a castle that would grace a fairy-tale. It can be a little overcrowded in summer, and the purist might argue it has rather too many tourist-based shops, but it is still worth every moment spent in it, having quiet corners where it is possible to get away from the crowds.

The best place to start an exploration is the car park at the southern (A39) end of the village, where there is a Visitor Centre for the National Park. The Somerset Guild of Craftsmen has a gallery here. The tower to the north-west is **Conygar Tower**, built in 1776 by a member of the Luttrell family, lords of the manor, for the mighty sum of £192. It is named from the hill on which it stands (itself named for the rabbit warren which existed here in medieval times) and is a folly in the grand style, having been built for no better reason than to create a landmark.

From the car park walk down High Street to reach the **Yarn Market**, a wonderful building built in the first years of the seventeenth century by

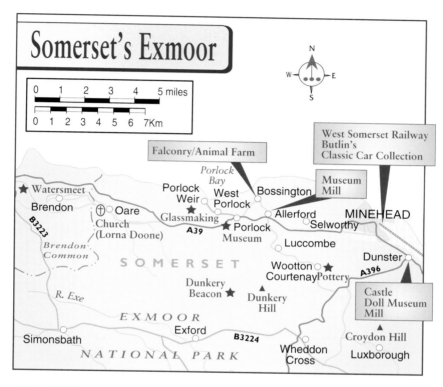

Somerset's Exmoor

N
W — E
S

0   1   2   3   4   5 miles
0 1 2 3 4 5 6 7Km

Falconry/Animal Farm

West Somerset Railway
Butlin's
Classic Car Collection

Porlock Bay

Museum
Mill

Watersmeet
Brendon
Oare
Church
(Lorna Doone)

Porlock
Weir
West
Porlock
Glassmaking
A39
Porlock
Museum

Bossington

Allerford
Selworthy

MINEHEAD

B3223

Brendon Common

Luccombe

Dunster

S O M E R S E T

R. Exe

Wootton
Courtenay Pottery

A396

Dunkery
Beacon

Dunkery
Hill

Castle
Doll Museum
Mill

E X M O O R

Simonsbath

Exford

B3224

Croydon Hill

N A T I O N A L   P A R K

Wheddon
Cross

Luxborough

the Luttrells as a market for cloth when the village was a centre for the local wool trade. The market was damaged in 1647 during the Civil War, some roofing timber still showing the impact marks of a cannonball. The restoration work is commemorated in the weather vane, which is marked 'GL1647'. GL is George Luttrell. Opposite the market is the **Luttrell Arms Hotel**, built in about 1500 as either a guest house for Cleeve Abbey or a town house for the Abbot. After the Dissolution the Luttrells bought the abbey's house and the two beside it and remodelled them into the Ship Inn. The name changed sometime in the mid-eighteenth century.

About half-way down High Street, on the right, is the **Dunster Dolls Museum**, which has a good collection of antique and ethnic dolls. The collection was started by a local resident and presented to the village on her death. A burglary in 1990 resulted in the loss of some of the most interesting dolls, but the collection is still worth visiting. At the bottom of the High Street the **castle** is straight ahead.

There is a legend that a Celtic fort stood here and was used by the Celtic St Carantoc to exhibit a dragon that he had charmed from the sea on the orders of King Arthur. It is known that Aluric, a Saxon, built a castle here, and it is likely that a Norman castle was built on the same site. Of that first Norman building only a tower and part of a curtain wall remain, though there are other sections of the building that represent additions from the thirteenth century. One addition was the gatehouse, a formidable structure, one tower of which was known to have been used as a dungeon.

Civil War action

The castle saw service during the Civil War when it was twice besieged. At first it was held for Parliament and withstood a Royalist siege in 1642 before the Luttrells changed sides in 1643. In 1645 it was besieged again, this time by Parliament. The siege lasted for six months, until long after all other West Country castles had surrendered and the King's cause was hopeless. Then starvation caused the castle garrison to surrender, though they found the strength to march out with honour. Acknowledging the castle's great strength as a fortress, Cromwell had the castle slighted, a semi-demolition that included the razing of the original Norman keep.

In Victorian times the whole building was re-structured as a domestic building. Inside, the castle is a fine mix of Elizabethan and later work, with wood panelling and plaster ceilings and, in the Leather Gallery, some remarkable leather 'tapestries'. One room was used by the Prince of Wales, later Charles II, during a stay in 1645 when the Civil War was going badly for his father. Equally good are the castle gardens that include, among the more unusual plants, orange and lemon trees, camellias and magnolias. Dunster Castle is now administered by the National Trust.

At the bottom of High Street bear right into Church Street, passing, to the right, the **Nunnery**, a superb, triple-storey, double-overhung building. Despite the name there was never a house of nuns in Dunster, the building dating from the mid-fourteenth century when it was built as a guest house for Cleeve Abbey. The building is now three private cottages. Next on the right are the village gardens – once part of the Priory and later the walled kitchen garden for the castle – and the church. **St George's Church** dates from the early 1400s when the earlier priory church was reconstructed (some early work still remains). The crossing tower was added in 1443 by a local stonemason. Inside there are several monuments to members of the Luttrell family, but the most interesting memorial is the cover slab from the grave of Adam of Cheddar, Dunster's prior in the mid-fourteenth century.

THE VILLAGERS AND THE MONKS

A Benedictine priory was built in Dunster in the early twelfth century, but very unusually the Priory Church was shared between the village and the monks. Eventually a dispute arose over the times of service and use of bells, coming to a head when the villagers removed the bell ropes so that the monks could not toll them. The incensed prior wrote that 'to fulfill and satisfie theire croked appetites, thei take up the bell roopis and said that the Priour and convent there should have no bellis there to ryng'. The dispute was taken to Glastonbury where an unsatisfactory decision was reached that the building should be divided into two. That decision resulted in one of the longest rood screens in Britain, over 50ft (16m) long and massively constructed. The screen was built locally and erected in 1499.

To the right, beyond the church, St George's Street leads to the **Butter Cross** and the **Dovecote**. The Butter Cross is thought to have been the original village market cross, perhaps moved here when plague was rife so that local farmers did not need to enter the village. The dovecote is part of the remains of Dunster Priory. The charming round building, with a conical slate roof topped by what for all the world is an up-market bird-table, had nesting spaces for 500 pairs of doves. It still has its original revolving ladder for reaching the nests. Opposite the dovecote is the village's sixteenth-century tithe barn.

Bear left along West Street. First left is Mill Lane at the end of which is **Dunster Water Mill** dating from the seventeenth century. The mill was restored in 1979 and still grinds flour for local bakeries. Visitors can watch the process (and buy flour), see a collection of old agricultural machinery or enjoy the tea room. The mill is now owned by the National Trust.

The second left, Park Street, leads to **Gallox Bridge**, a fine medieval packhorse bridge. The name is believed to be a corruption of gallows, a name borrowed from the hill to the south. Legend has it that after Judge Jeffreys' Bloody Assize, which followed the Monmouth Rebellion and the battle of Sedgemoor, a gallows was erected under the hill and two (perhaps three) local men were hanged. However, some experts believe the gallows of the name probably existed long before the rebellion. A very fine walk climbs the hill and then circles Dunster Park, visiting

Bat's Castle, an Iron Age hillfort. An equally good walk climbs Grabbist Hill to the west of the village.

MINEHEAD

Nunnery, Dunster

To the west of Dunster, and just outside the National Park, is **Minehead**, the major holiday centre of Somerset Exmoor. The town's curious name is thought to derive from the Celtic (Welsh) *mynydd*, hill, as the original town grew up on the flanks of North Hill which offered shelter from the prevailing wind. Three distinct sections of the town emerged and these can still be detected. Higher Town is the old section, on the flank of North Hill. Below it, Lower Town grew up around the market, which was placed, for convenience, at the base of the hill. Bottom, or Quay, Town grew up around the harbour.

Higher Town is the most picturesque part of Minehead, particularly Church Steps, a steep line of steps that rises between thatched cottages to the thirteenth/fourteenth-century **St Michael's Church**. Inside there is a fine fifteenth-century rood screen similar to that at Dunster. Lower Town was centred on the market that was held in what is now The Parade. There was a market from the early fifteenth century, but an annual fair a hundred years earlier. There is still a market in Minehead, held weekly on Tuesdays and Thursdays next to the railway station. In Market House Lane, off The Parade, close to the imposing Town Hall, are the town's **Almshouses**, built in 1630

by Robert Quirke. Heading towards the sea from The Parade, a left turn into Blenheim Road leads to the Blenheim Gardens, opened in 1925 and still one of the joys of the town. Close to The Parade is the Exmoor Classic Car Collection, recently moved to the town from Yorkshire. This private collection of cars, motor cycles and memorabilia is amazing.

Bottom Town was centred on the harbour at the western end of the bay, tucked under Culver Cliff. In Quay Street, which leads to the harbour, there are fine thatched cottages. Minehead's harbour was prosperous in medieval times, the trade being mainly cross-channel with Wales, but also including significant fish exports to Ireland. By the seventeenth century the Minehead fishing fleet, netting cod off Newfoundland, was a source of great wealth, but silting gradually reduced the trade. In 1791 a fire burnt down much of Lower Town and the town did not recover. Only with the advent of seaside holidays and the arrival of the railway did the town really take off. Walking along The Esplanade from the harbour the typical structure of an English seaside resort can be seen. The railway station is now the terminus of the **West Somerset Railway**.

Yarn Market, Dunster

Shopping in Minehead and the Church Steps Minehead

THE WHISTLING GHOST OF SUSANNA LEAKEY

Susanna Leakey, a Minehead widow, died in 1634 but, it seems, continued to look out for the interests of her son Alexander. He was a Minehead ship owner and the ghost of his mother was said to appear every time one of his ships was sighted, whistling up a wind to blow the ship safely home. The ghostly whistle became such a feature of the town that in 1637 William Piers, the Bishop of Bath and Wells, came down to investigate. His conclusion was that 'there never was any such apparition at all'.

WEST SOMERSET RAILWAY

The West Somerset is the longest private railway in the country. The railway was begun in 1857, Isambard Kingdom Brunel being the first engineer, but did not reach Minehead until 1874. It was absorbed into the Great Western Railway company in 1897 and fell victim to Dr Beeching's axe in 1971. Private services began in 1976. The line runs for just over 20 miles (30kms) to Bishops Lydeard, with stations at Dunster, Blue Anchor, Washford, Watchet, Doniford Halt, Williton, Stogumber and Crowcombe Heathfield. The journey is through superb Somerset scenery, a great outing as all trains are steam-hauled.

Beyond the station the town's seafront continues with the usual array of amusements and cafés, and leads to **Butlins Family Entertainment Resort**, built on marshland in the early 1960s. The original Butlins has been updated, its facilities extended to cater for modern holidaymakers. Day and half-day tickets to the site are available. Inside there are entertainments too numerous to list and with frequently changing themes.

THE MINEHEAD HOBBY HORSE

Despite the overt commercialism which is a requirement of a successful British seaside resort, Minehead retains its character, not only in its hillside village and old port, but in its 'Somerset-town' heart, a fact that is reinforced by its being the only town in the county which celebrates Mayday morning with a hobby horse. In fact there are two horses: the Sailor's Horse is the oldest, being recorded from at least the early nineteenth century, while the Town

Horse was added to the festivities in 1903.

BELOW DUNKERY BEACON

To the west of Minehead a 'no through road' leads over Bratton Ball (ball is the local dialect word for a rounded hill) and on towards Selworthy Beacon. From several points on this road, and at its end, there are terrific views along the coast. This is also good walking country: the South-West Coast Path, Britain's longest National Trail starts (or ends) at Minehead's harbour and runs parallel to the road.

To explore Exmoor from Minehead, take the A39 westwards. After the extensive plantation of Great Headon, to the left, there is a turn, also left, to **Wootton Courtenay**, a delightful village where the Domesday mill site is now occupied by a later mill in which Michael Gaitskell produces a distinctive range of stoneware. Minor roads from the village reach the A396. They also offer a chance to walk on the east side, the rarely visited side, of Dunkery Hill, though parking can be a problem.

The next left is for Luccombe, but ignore that village for the present to reach Selworthy by taking the next right turn. **Selworthy** is a village of whitewashed, thatched cottages, largely built by Sir Thomas Acland for retired workers from his Holnicote Estate (now owned by the National Trust). The village church is also whitewashed, giving it a curious, fairy-tale quality that merely adds to the dream-like, timelessness of the village. The church tower dates from the fourteenth century, much of the rest from two hundred years later. From the church there are marvellous views of high Exmoor. From the village a fine walk heads north through mixed deciduous – with evergreen oak and some conifer – woodland to reach Bury Castle, another Iron Age hillfort. The walk can be extended to Selworthy Beacon for fine coastal views.

The next village on the right is **Allerford**, not as pretty as Selworthy perhaps, but very attractive, particularly near the old packhorse bridge where ducks encourage visitors to part with their lunch. There is a small museum in the old village school: a Victorian classroom has been reproduced, there are items reflecting the rural life of the area at about the same time and a photographic archive. Across the main road from Allerford is **Piles Mill**, probably named for Edward Pyle, a miller in the sixteenth century. From Allerford a road leads to picturesque Bossington where **Bossington Farm** has a pets' corner and pony rides, and a collection of birds of prey (owls and falcons). There are frequent flying displays. From Bossington an excellent walk visits Hurlstone Point for a fine view over Porlock Bay.

Now turn next left from the A39, passing through **West Luccombe**, where there is another lovely packhorse bridge to reach **Horner**, a beautiful, if somewhat over-crowded in summer, little village lying in the wooded valley of Horner Water, over which there is also a packhorse bridge.

The village is associated with the Acland family who rose from humble beginnings in the fifteenth century to owning so much land that it was said they could ride from

Porlock to Exeter without ever going over one of their own boundaries. Thanks to the magnificent gesture of Sir Richard Acland the 12,400 acres of the Holnicote (pronounced Honey-cut) Estate were given to the National Trust in 1944. The family lived in Holnicote House, beside the A39 opposite the turn to Selworthy. The next village is **Luccombe**, equally as attractive as its neighbours and with an impressively large church for such a small place.

The Loyal Vicar of Luccombe

At the outbreak of the Civil War the vicar of Luccombe was Henry Byam, an outspoken supporter of the king. The vicar had four sons; all served in the Royalist army and two of them were killed fighting. Byam was himself imprisoned, but escaped and joined the future Charles II on his flight to France. Byam's wife and only daughter followed him, but were drowned when their ship was lost in a storm. Despite these tribulations Byam returned to Luccombe at the Restoration and served as vicar until 1669 when he died aged 89.

HIGHEST EXMOOR

There are fine walks from these little villages, particularly along Horner Water from Horner, through the woodland to the south-west of Luccombe and also from Webber's Post, on the minor road which climbs the flank of Dunkery Hill from Horner/Luccombe. From walks in the woodland by the post car park there are spectacular views of Horner Hill and the local valleys. For most walkers, though, the main objective is **Dunkery Beacon**, Exmoor's highest point, which can be comfortably climbed from one of the small car parks on the minor road.

DUNKERY BEACON

The name Dunkery is said to derive from the Celtic *dun creagh*, a rocky hill, which is about as inappropriate a name as could be imagined. It is almost easier to believe the story of the Devil creating the hill with the shovelful of earth he removed from the Punchbowl near Winsford. The 'Beacon' was added after successive signal fires, the earliest of which could perhaps go back to very ancient times. Of late, beacon fires have been built here to commemorate the Queen's Coronation and Jubilee, Royal weddings and to celebrate the centenary of the publication of *Lorna Doone*.

The summit is crowned with a huge cairn, a trig point and a toposcope pointing out details of the view. On a good day this takes in the Mendips to the north-east, the Brecon Beacons to the north, and Dartmoor and Bodmin Moor to the south, as well as the Brendons and the Quantocks, the sea and, of course, the superb local scenery, most especially the valley of Horner Water and Horner Wood. The local high moor here is surprisingly prolific in wildflowers. The list includes not only bell heather, bilberry and gorse, as might be expected, but also tormentil, blue heather speedwell, heath spotted orchid, bog pimpernel and milkwort.

The ridge of moor, of which Dunkery is the highest point, was almost certainly a trackway in ancient times and the burial mounds along it indicate its importance in the Bronze Age. A fine ridge top walk visits the mounds of Great and Little Rowbarrow. On the other side

The Summit of Dunkery Beacon

ERECTED IN
SEPTEMBER 1935
TO COMMEMORATE
THE HANDING OVER TO
THE
NATIONAL TRUST
FOR PLACES OF
HISTORIC INTEREST
OR
NATURAL BEAUTY
OF
DUNKERY HILL
FOR
THE BENEFIT OF THE NATION
BY
SIR THOMAS ACLAND Bt.
COLONEL WIGGIN
AND
ALLAN HUGHES ESQ.

of the Dunkery Hill, across the minor road are the mounds of Robin How and Joaney How. The names are nineteenth-century inventions, the word 'how' being derived from

Porlock Weir

BLACKMORE AND LORNA DOONE

Richard Doddridge Blackmore was born in 1825, the son of John Blackmore, the curate of Longworth, Berkshire but sadly his mother died soon after and much of the responsibility for his up-bringing fell to his grandparents, his grandfather – also John – being the rector of Oare church. Richard was boarded at Blundells School, Tiverton and spent holidays here on Exmoor, learning at first hand the old stories of the Doones, a seventeenth-century family of local outlaws. Richard qualified as a barrister after graduating from Oxford but when ill-health forced him to give up his practice he turned to writing full time. Though he lived in Middlesex he retained an affection for Exmoor, visiting frequently before his death in 1900. Lorna Doone remains Blackmore's most popular book.

Considerable research has now been carried out on the story of Lorna Doone, and it is now established that the book is partly factual, though elaborated to create a compelling drama. It is, therefore, 'faction' rather than fact or fiction. Research suggests that a very small group of Scots under the leadership of a knight of Clan Stewart were outlawed in the early years of the seventeenth century as a result of a family feud. The head of the group, Sir James Stewart, took the Gaelic, poetic version of his name when he settled in a remote Exmoor valley, calling himself Iain Ciar Duine but retaining his knightly 'Sir'. The locals, not understanding the Gaelic, called him Sir Ensor Doone and the name stuck.

The lands that Sir Ensor had lost were those of Lorne in North Argyll. In his Exmoor valley Sir Ensor's sons grew up to become real outlaws, holding the county to ransom, while Sir Ensor dreamed of recapturing his former wealth and title. In an attempt to do so he kidnapped the daughter of the new lords, with the intention of marrying her to his eldest son, Charles, (Carver) when she came of age. To hide her identity she was called Lorna (from her lands) Doone.

It was this girl that John Ridd, a real man of Blackmore's time, who truly was a local wrestling champion, met when he climbed the water-slide one day. In the story John marries Lorna, the Doones are defeated and their village burned. Then John and Lorna live happily ever after. Some suggest that most of this is also true, the Doones leaving Exmoor to return to Scotland and Lorna staying locally even when her true identity was known. As records from Oare church do not go back far enough no marriage record exists, so it is not definite that John and Lorna really did marry. Only in one respect did Blackmore positively alter the story and that was in moving it twenty years forward to 1665 so that the author could weave in some local intrigue about Monmouth's rebellion and Judge Jeffreys' Assize: these latter dates could not be altered.

the Norse word for a barrow. The first names are harder to pin down, but it is speculated that they may be from Robin Hood and Little John who are often associated with such places. It may seem a long way from Sherwood Forest, but there is another, and distinct, use of Robin Hood's name near Taunton.

The minor road descends the flank of Dunkery Hill to Dunkery Bridge and Gate, then continues to reach the B324 close to **Wheddon Cross** with its welcoming inn, but notorious cross-roads. Here, **Barle Valley Safaris** offer on and off-road trips exploring the natural history of the moor.

PORLOCK TO OARE

Back on the A39, the next village is **Porlock**, famous for its hill. Porlock is an attractive village despite the main road that bisects it. It is known that Vikings landed here in 914 and that a Saxon army landed in 1052, so clearly the village was a major port in Saxon times. Today it lies over $1/_2$ mile (1km) from the sea as a result of the silting of Porlock Bay. The **Dovery Manor Museum** in the High Street explores the village's history. The house is late fifteenth-century, but seems never to have been the manor house, despite the name. The Ship Inn, close to the base of Porlock Hill, dates from at least the sixteenth century. Robert Southey wrote a sonnet and Coleridge part of *The Rime of the Ancient Mariner* here.

In another village inn, the Rose and Crown, now a private house opposite the church, Blackmore stayed while researching facts for *Lorna Doone*. The church, dedicated to St Dubricius (or Dyfrig), a sixth-century Celtic saint, has a curiously truncated, oak-shingled spire. It is said that it lost its top during a storm around 1700. Inside is the memorial of Baron Harrington who fought with Henry V at Agincourt. From the village, Discovery Safaris run Landrovers in search of red deer and other delights of the National Park.

To the west from the village is **Porlock Weir**, a picturesque small harbour, the launching point for the Lynmouth lifeboat during the epic rescue of the *Forest Hall* (see Chapter 3).

At Exmoor Glass visitors can watch a range of glassware being handblown.

Southwards from Porlock a difficult road rises to **Stoke Pero** where stands one of the highest and remote churches on Exmoor. One tale, probably apocryphal, recounts a visitor asking at Porlock for the best way to Stoke Pero and being told that there was no best way. By the late nineteenth century the church was ruinous but the Acland family of Holnicote Estate paid for its restoration. This was carried out in 1896-97: roofing timber had to be brought from Porlock and was carried by a donkey called Zulu who made the trip twice daily for months. As a reward, Zulu has his portrait hanging inside the church, which if not unique, is certainly unusual.

The A39 climbs Porlock Hill, then crosses magnificent moorland. A road to the left crosses the moor to Exford, passing an ancient stone row and circle. The next left descends to the Weir Water, a lovely valley that leads to Oare. But after that junction the road passes one interesting site on the northern (coast) side. Best reached on foot, and lying on the Coast Path, is **Culbone Church** which has the curious distinction of being noted in the Guinness Book of Records. This records Culbone as England's smallest parish church. The church is just over 35ft(10m) long, the nave not quite $12^1/_2$ft (4m) wide, and is exquisitely sited on a wooded hillside.

THE MAN OF PORLOCK AND *KUBLA KHAN*

In the summer of 1797 Samuel Taylor Coleridge, at that time living on the Quantocks, took a cottage (probably the now-demolished Withycombe Farm) above the sea near Culbone in an attempt to shake off ill health. Coleridge was known to have been taking laudanum and may also have taken other drugs to alleviate his symptoms. Whatever the cause he fell into a deep sleep while reading a book on Kubla Khan and awoke after about three hours with his poem on the great Mongol leader fully formed in his head. He immediately began to transcribe the poem, but when he had completed only 54 lines there was a knock at the door. It was the 'Man of Porlock' who had come on some trivial matter and spent an hour with the increasingly frustrated poet. By the time he had left Coleridge had forgotten the verse and so lost the thread that the poem remained unfinished. It remains a 54-line masterpiece.

DOONE COUNTRY

Oare can be reached along the Weir Water road, which crosses the picturesque Robber's Bridge, or on the direct route from the A39. The

Domesday Book refers to Oare (as Are) but it is not known whether there was a church here before the present building was constructed in the fourteenth century. The tower is later, having been built in the mid-nineteenth century when the church was also extended – a fact that helps the Lorna Doone story.

Within the church, most visitors are looking for the

Oare church

window through which Lorna was shot and it is dutifully marked with a card. But the book does not actually specify that Lorna was shot through a window. If Carver Doone had shot her along the length of the

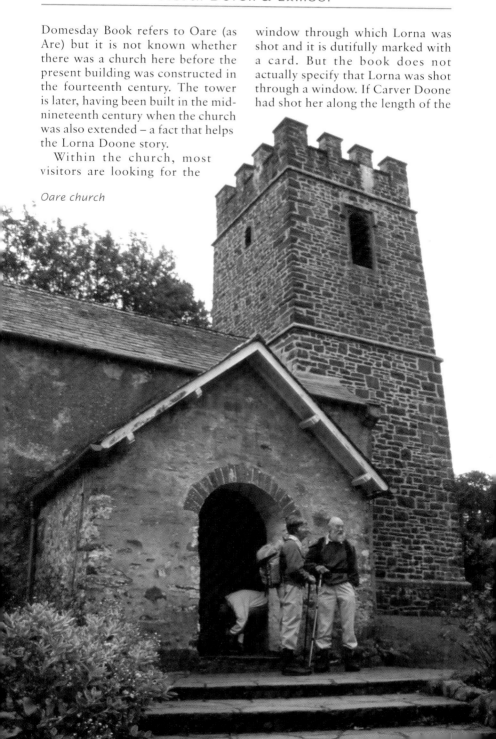

church he would probably have walked away such was his reputation. Nevertheless, the fact that the church has been extended means that where the altar would have been in the seventeenth century would have left a bride visible from the moor's edge through the southern window. The church also has a fine memorial tablet to RD Blackmore.

Look, too, for the piscina. It is in the shape of a head held by a pair of hands, a representation of the final act of the Celtic St Decuman whose story we have heard at Watchet. The piscina represents that final part of the tale when the saint's body carried its severed head to a holy well to wash it.

The Exmoor of Lorna Doone

Oare will be forever associated with Lorna Doone, but there are other places that occur in the book that can be identified. Lorna Doone Farm was the residence of Nicholas Snowe, the churchwarden: parts of the building are believed to be over 1000 years old. Opposite the church is Oare House, possibly the model for John Ridd's Plover's Barrows Farm. Robber's Bridge is where John Ridd's father was murdered. Badgworthy Water, the county boundary between Somerset and Devon, is the book's Bagworthy Water, where young John Ridd went fishing. The locals pronounce the stream's name 'badgery' which explains the spelling change. The water-slide (it is definitely more a slide than a falls, despite the exaggerations of several films of the book) is at the entrance to Lank Combe, in which are the ruins of medieval cottages, probably the old homes of Sir Ensor and Carver Doone, though there are also the remains of houses in Hoccombe, the next valley to the south.

To reach Badgworthy Water the footpath beside Oare church is followed to Cloud Farm. Beyond the farm, turn left beside the stream, passing a memorial stone to RD Blackmore and continuing to reach the waterslide and Lank Combe, to the right (and, therefore, in Devon). Hoccombe is reached soon after, also to the right.

Back on the A39 the visitor soon reaches County Gate and the boundary of Somerset and Devon.

Places to Visit

Somerset's Exmoor

Dunster Dolls Museum

High Street
Open: Easter-October, Monday-Friday 10.30am-4.30pm, Saturday and Sunday 2-5pm. ☎ 01643 821220

Dunster Castle (NT)

Open: Castle: Easter-October, Saturday-Wednesday 11am-5pm (4pm in October).
Garden and Park: April-September, daily 10am-5pm; January-March and October-December, daily 11am-4pm.
Closed Christmas Day and Boxing Day.
☎ 01643 821314

Places to Visit

Dunster Water Mill (NT)

Open: April-October, daily 10.30am-5pm (closed Friday April-June and October). ☎ 01643 821759

Somerset Guild of Craftsmen

Dunster Steep, Dunster
Open: All year daily 10am-4.30pm.
☎ 01643 821 235

Exmoor Classic Car Collection

Parkhouse Road, Minehead
Open: Easter-September, Tuesday-Thursday 11am-4pm.
☎ 01643 841476 or 07970 497741

West Somerset Railway

The Railway Station, Minehead
Open: Open throughout the year, except in November and with limited services December-March. From June-September there are up to 8 trains daily in both directions.
☎ 01643 704996

Butlins Family Entertainment Resort

Minehead
Open: May-October, daily 9.30am-6pm (Last entry 4pm).
☎ 01643 708171

Mill Pottery

Wootton Courtenay
Open: April-December, Tuesday-Saturday 10am-1pm, 2-5.30pm. Also open Sundays and Mondays by appointment and most days in January-March – but ring to make sure. ☎ 01643 841297

West Somerset Rural Life Museum

Allerford
Open: Good Friday-October, Monday-Friday 10.30am-1pm, 2-4.30pm. Also open on Sundays 2-4.30pm from mid-July-early September. ☎ 01643 862529

Exmoor Falconry and Animal Farm

Bossington Farm, Nr Allerford
Open: November-February, daily except Sunday 10.30am-4pm.
☎ 01643 862816

Barle Valley Safaris

Station Cottage, Goosemoor
Wheddon Cross
Open: All year daily. Halfday, day and evening safaris.
☎ 01643 851386

Dovery Manor Museum

High Street, Porlock
Open: May-September, Monday-Friday 10am-1pm, 2-5pm. Saturday 10am-12noon, 2-4pm.
☎ 01643 863150

Discovery Safaris

Porlock
Open: Tours at 2pm most days. Also evenings June-September
☎ 01643 863080 or 07957 721568

Exmoor Glass

Porlock Weir
Open: All year daily 10am-5pm (Glass blowing Monday-Saturday)
☎ 01643 863141

3. Devon's Exmoor

The western section of the Exmoor National Park, that section which lies within Devon, is subtly different in character to Somerset Exmoor. There are still excellent sections of moor, but it is lower and the coast is more rugged.

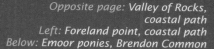

Devon's Exmoor

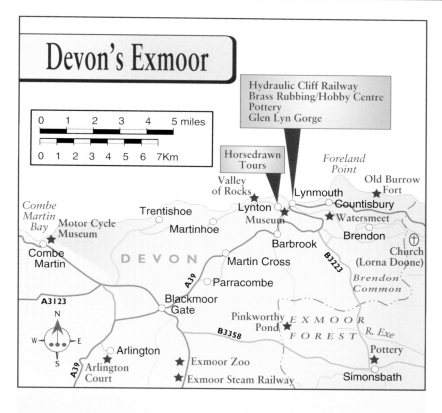

Hydraulic Cliff Railway
Brass Rubbing/Hobby Centre
Pottery
Glen Lyn Gorge

| 0 | 1 | 2 | 3 | 4 | 5 miles |

| 0 | 1 | 2 | 3 | 4 | 5 | 6 | 7Km |

Horsedrawn Tours

Foreland Point

Valley of Rocks

Lynmouth

Old Burrow Fort

Combe Martin Bay

Trentishoe

Lynton
Museum

Countisbury

Motor Cycle Museum

Martinhoe

Watersmeet

Brendon

Combe Martin

Barbrook

Church (Lorna Doone)

D E V O N

Martin Cross

B3223

A39

Parracombe

Brendon Common

A3123

Blackmoor Gate

Pinkworthy Pond

E X M O O R

N

W — E

B3358

F O R E S T

R. Exe

S

Arlington

Pottery

A39

Arlington Court

★ Exmoor Zoo

Simonsbath

★ Exmoor Steam Railway

COUNTISBURY AND BRENDON COMMON

At County Gate, on the border between the two counties there is a car park and National Park Information Centre. The view from the car park is marvellous, taking in the valley of Badgworthy Water and, to its right as you look, the high moor of **Brendon Common**. There are fine walks from County Gate. One of the best heads back into Somerset to climb Sugarloaf, named for its shape by the Rev Walter Halliday who founded the Glenthorne Estate on which the peak stands. Sugarloaf is one of the best viewpoints along the Exmoor coast. Another good walk visits the **Old Burrow fort**, to the north-west of County Gate.

OLD BURROW FORT

The hill is topped by a small Roman fort probably built very early after the Roman invasion as a coastal look-out. The fort consisted of a roughly circular, double ditch and rampart defence about 328 ft (100m) across surrounding a rectangular ditch and rampart inner fort about 92 x 85ft (28 x 26m). The entrance to the inner fort was set on the opposite side from that to the outer fort, and protected by a wooden tower. No foundations from permanent buildings have been found inside the fort, so it is thought that the defenders lived in tents. However, a large field oven has been found. Coins found at the site suggest only a three- or four-year Roman presence and it is thought that the fort was used to support operations by troop ships against the Silures of South Wales, a Celtic tribe who held up the Roman conquest of Britain for several years. It is not clear whether Old Burrow was abandoned (in about 54AD) when the Silures were subdued or simply because the similar fort at Martinhoe, about 8 miles (13km) to the west, offered a better view or better local weather for viewing.

To the west the first left turn from the A39 visits the hamlets of Brendon and Leeford, which are wonderfully picturesque. The village church is over 2 miles (3.2km) to the west.

ST BRENDAN'S CHURCH

In 1738 the inhabitants of the farms, villages and hamlets around Brendon and Cheriton decided to reposition the church for the benefit of all. They took it down, stone by stone and rebuilt it further to the west, but still in a very isolated position. Unfortunately it was later 'restored' by the Victorians, though some interesting pieces remain, a Norman font and a sundial dated 1707.

After Monmouth's rebellion, Nathaniel Wade, who had been one of the Duke's commanders at Sedgemoor, attempted to escape by boat along the Bristol Channel – apparently choosing to embark at Ilfracombe. He sailed up-channel, a curious direction – but was forced ashore near Lynmouth by bad weather. Heading inland, he was hidden by John Birch, the farmer of Farley Water Farm near where St Brendan's then stood. His occasional movements were spotted by the rector of St Brendan's who alerted the authorities. John Birch, fearing torture and execution, hanged himself, but Wade, captured and tried, was pardoned.

From Brendon/Leeford a minor road climbs to Cross Gate. From here walkers can explore Brendon

The Great Porlock Rescue

On 12 January 1899 the *Forest Hall* got into difficulties in Porlock Bay
and a call went out to launch the Lynmouth lifeboat. Unfortunately the
sea was swamping the slipway and launching was impossible, but the
coxswain, Jack Crocombe, decided to haul the boat to Porlock for
launching there. Helped by his crew, a team of horses, and most of the
population of Lynton and Lynmouth, Jack hauled the 3¹/₂ ton boat – a 10-
oared boat called *Louisa* – up Countisbury Hill on its wheeled launcher
carriage. At the top they found a section of moorland road to be too
narrow for the carriage, so the boat was taken off and hauled through on
skids while the carriage went through fields to the lane's end. The
journey of 15 miles (24km) to Porlock, which also required a section of
wall beside the road to be dismantled, was completed in about 13 hours,
overnight, in appalling weather. The boat was launched immediately, at
7am, and successfully reached the *Forest Hall*. Each of the men on the
Louisa's crew, one of whom was only sixteen years old, received a silver
watch as a memento. A sister boat of the *Louisa* can be seen at Lynmouth.

Common. (As noted earlier, the
name here possibly derives from
'broom', the plant and not from
'brown hills' as for the Brendon
Hills.) A very good walk approaches
Doone country from above.

Back on the A39 the next place
of interest is **Countisbury**, famous
for the hill that descends from it and
for the Exmoor Sandpiper Inn, but
were it not for the church, barely
big enough to warrant being called
a hamlet. Inside the church are the
clappers from the bells, all that was
salvaged when the bells were sold
for the upkeep of the building.
There is also a notice that points out
that many of the crew of the *Louisa*
are buried in the churchyard.

From the church take the path
towards the cliffs. **Butter Hill** is
topped by an ancient signal station,
now in use again. The view from the
hill is excellent in all directions, but
especially westward past Wind Hill
to Lynmouth and the coast beyond.

LYNMOUTH

Lynmouth, at the foot of Countisbury
Hill, is a prettily set old fishing village, though today it is largely given
over to tourism. The landmarks of
the town lie close to the harbour.
The **Rhenish Tower** was built early
in the nineteenth century by Gen-
eral Rawdon as a lighthouse for the
harbour and to store sea water that
was used in his bath! Rawdon is said
to have modelled it on a tower he
had seen on the Lebanese coast, but
it is named for its similarity to tow-
ers on the Rhine. The tower is actually a replica, the original having
been destroyed in 1952.

Across from the tower is one of
Lynmouth's most appealing features, the **Cliff Railway**. In the mid-
nineteenth century the huge and
steep hill from Lynmouth to Lynton
was adversely affecting the tourist
trade. A local engineer, Bob Jones,
therefore decided to build a cliff

Above: **Countisbury Church**

Above and right: **Lynmouth cliff railway**

Below: **Lynmouth**

Opposite page: **Rhenish tower, Lynmouth**

railway to increase trade and on Easter Monday 1890 the railway was ready.

It rises 450ft in 900ft (metric measures do not seem right for something so delightfully Imperial), the motive power being the carriages themselves. Beneath each one is a 700-gallon water tank. The carriage at the top has its tank filled and it then hauls the lower carriage up. At the bottom the tank is emptied, while the top tank is filled again. The trip takes about $1\frac{1}{2}$ minutes and on the first day cost three old pence up and two old pence down. Bob Jones' original design for hydraulic and emergency brakes was so good that despite the railway having transported million s of passengers, no one has ever been injured – though a dog once had its tail shortened when it wandered on to the track. In the same year as the railway opened, water from the East Lyn River was piped to the local generating station giving Lynmouth and Lynton electricity before many places in London had been connected.

Near the railway's bottom station are two old lime kilns, Lynmouth having once been a centre for lime-burning. Lime was shipped in from South Wales, burned here and moved up on to Exmoor to 'sweeten' the soil. Next to the kilns, part of the old Pavilion (where entertainments took place in the early years of tourism) now houses a National Park Visitor Centre. The sistership of the lifeboat *Louisa* is displayed here.

Walking away from the sea the visitor reaches the **Flood Memorial Hall** where the story of the 1952 disaster is told.

The Lyn Flood

In the first two weeks of August 1952 rain fell almost continually on Exmoor, raising the levels of the Hoar Oak, and the East and West Lyn Rivers. Then on 15 August the rain worsened. That day was the third wettest ever recorded in Britain, with almost 12 inches of rain falling on Exmoor. The drainage area of the rivers collected 3,000 million gallons (about 90 million tons) of water and it poured downstream as a huge wave. The Lyn rivers are very steep, averaging about 1 in 27 along their length, and the effect of water-weight and gravity was devastating. Bridges, trees and buildings that were knocked over created temporary dams and when these failed the water surged and was even more powerful. With the water came an estimated 100,000 tons of rocks, some weighing 50 tons or more. When Lynmouth was struck it was washed away, daybreak revealing the loss of dozen of hotels and houses. Nineteen boats had been washed away, as had over 150 cars. Worst of all, 34 men, women and children had been killed.

The disaster brought assistance from all over the world: over £1.3 million (at 1952 prices) was collected for relief and in two years Lynmouth had been rebuilt. The story of the flood is told in the Flood Memorial Hall.

Continue beside the East Lyn to reach the junction of the two Lyn streams. Across Lyndale Bridge is the

Shelley's Cottage Hotel which reputedly stands on the site of the cottage of Miss Hooper, which was rented by the poet and his 16-year old wife Harriet Westbrook for their honeymoon. Shelley's trip was not wholly holiday as he was being pursued by the government for having distributed pamphlets rife with revolutionary thoughts. In 1812, with the Napoleonic wars still being fought, such behaviour was definitely suspect. During his stay Shelley worked on *Queen Mab*, but also continued to write the pamphlets, distributing them, in part, by the apparently useless method of putting them in bottles and throwing them in the sea. After a stay of many weeks a kindly Lynmouth fisherman took the poet across to South Wales when arrest was imminent.

Beyond the hotel – on the road for Watersmeet – **Exmoor's Brass Rubbing and Hobbycraft Centre** offers do-it-yourself (and ready-made) rubbings from 150 facsimiles of brasses dating from the thirteenth century and a range of local crafts, including some craft kits. Also in Watersmeet Road is the **Lynmouth Pottery** where the techniques of pot throwing and firing can be watched. Children can try their hand at the potter's wheel or at painting their own pot. Finally in Lynmouth, at the cross-roads is the entrance to the **Glen Lyn Gorge**, a scenically beautiful part of the West Lyn River that has been designated as a Site of Special Scientific Interest for its boulders moved by the flood. The site also has a Power of Water Exhibition, centred on a small hydro-electric power station and a collection of steam engines and water-operated models. The same company runs boat trips that explore the local coast.

WATERSMEET

From Lynmouth the A39 follows the wooded valley of the East Lyn River back towards the moor. This is a beautiful stretch of country, and visitors can enjoy it at closer quarters at **Watersmeet**, where the Hoar Oak Water meets the East Lyn, the National Trust's valley site. The whole of the riverside estate from Lynmouth to Watersmeet House was acquired over a period of years by the Rev WS Halliday, a man of means who also subscribed to what might be termed the 'Romantic View' of nature. In 1832 he built the House – which is now a National Trust shop and restaurant. Anciently, the area was home to charcoal burners and, as an old adit (horizontal shaft) opposite the House shows, one group of enthusiastic but unsuccessful iron ore miners. Today the whole area is a haven for plants and wildlife, including Irish Spurge, Watersmeet being one of only two mainland British sites where this grows.

Beyond Watersmeet the main road continues through an equally magnificent wooded valley to reach a junction. The A39 bends sharply right here to reach Lynton, while the B3223 bears left, rising through the last of the woodland to reach open moor. The road across this excellent section of moorland, with Brendon Common to the left, has numerous parking places from which the moorland edge can be explored. The road verge at Brendon Two Gates is a popular starting point for walkers. The road eventually reaches Simonsbath.

Above: Watersmeet, near Lynmouth

Below: Coastal path, Foreland Point

The Hoar Oak

One very good walk from Brendon Two Gates visits the Hoar Oak (at Grid Reference 748430). The current tree was planted in 1917 to replace one planted in 1662 by James Boevey. Boevey's planting replaced an earlier tree, which marked a point on the boundary of the Royal Forest of Exmoor (the name derives from *har*, the old word for a boundary), but also showed solidarity with the recently enthroned Charles II. The use of an oak tree was probably a gesture to the famous incident when Charles I hid in an oak to escape capture, but oak is altogether the wrong sort of tree for so high and exposed a site. The nearby, flourishing beeches put the Hoar Oak to shame.

Those wanting to extend their walk can follow the Two Moors Way or the Tarka Trail (which are coincident for a while), heading north along the Cheriton Ridge before descending to the hamlet of Cheriton. From here the trails bear left to follow Hoar Oak Water to Hillsford Bridge, close to the junction of the A39 and B3223. A fine alternative is to continue west from the tree, crossing The Chains to Pinkworthy Pond (see Chapter 4).

LYNTON AND THE VALLEY OF ROCKS

Following the A39 the visitor reaches Barbrook from where

Lynton is reached by a road which starts out beside the East Lyn: there is an alternative, direct route from Lynmouth for those not visiting Watersmeet, climbing the last of the trio of hills that were feared by the drivers of cars many years ago, before engines became powerful enough to take such slopes without flinching.

Although Lynton is mentioned (as Lintone) in the Domesday Book its early history is really that of Lynmouth, the folk on the hill making their living from the harbour, just as those at the hill's base did. Not until the 1900s, when the tourist trade arrived, did Lynton achieve any prominence, those wishing to enjoy Lynmouth needing to stay in Lynton as the lack of available flat land at the base of the hill limited development. Lynton's first hotel was built in 1807, but it was the arrival of Sir George Newnes, the publisher, who backed the building of the cliff railway to link the village with the sea – that spurred a growth in building and prosperity. A few years later a narrow-gauge railway linked Lynton to Barnstaple, allowing holidaymakers to arrive more easily. The railway finally closed in 1935, motor transport having overtaken the roundabout railway route.

From the end of the path from the top of the cliff railway a right turn passes the impressive **Town Hall**, another of Sir George Newnes' benefactions to reach the **Convent of the Poor Clares and the Church of the Holy Saviour**. The nuns came to Lynton in 1910, by way of Woodchester, to escape persecution in their previous house at Rennes in Brittany. From the path's end a left turn passes the **Valley of the Rocks Hotel** built in glorious style in the late nineteenth century on the site of the village's first hotel of 1807.

Just beyond is **St Mary's Church**, originally built in the thirteenth century, but 'restored' in the nineteenth. Inside there is a memorial to Hugh Wichehalse, whose family built Lee Abbey (see below) and were lords of the manor in the sixteenth century. Turn right opposite the church to reach Queen Street, once called Pig Hill, the name being changed to celebrate Queen Victoria's Jubilee. Now turn left along Market Flats to reach the delightful St Vincent's Cottage which houses the **Lyn and Exmoor Museum**. Here a typical Exmoor kitchen has been reproduced. There are also collections on local geology, archaeology and wildlife and a model of the Barnstaple to Lynton railway.

Close to Lynton – to the south, near Barbrook – West Ilkerton Farm offers horse drawn tours of Exmoor. Visitors ride in a wagon drawn by shire horses for a unique view of the moor.

Also close to Lynton lies the **Valley of Rocks**, one of the most scenically spectacular, and enigmatic sites in the area. There is a road through the Valley, but to savour its delights it is best to use one of the car parks and walk. Close to the roundabout at the western end of the Valley are the best of the rock features. The **Devil's Cheesewring** is so-called because of its similarity to a cider press (the residue dry apple left after squeezing was known locally as cheese). **Rugged Jack** is said to be a local man petrified for drinking on a Sunday, while the nearby **Chimney Rock** is reputed to have been used by wreckers who shone a light from its top to lure ships on to the rocks below. **Castle Rock** is claimed to have been the site of a Celtic castle whose inhabitants were continuously plagued by the Devil. Only when they built Lynton's first church did he leave them in peace. Castle Rock can be easily climbed (Robert Southey, the poet, who fell in love with the Valley, climbed it in 1799 'with some toil') for a marvellous view of the sun setting into the Atlantic.

From the roundabout an improbable walk – **North Walk** – has been carved into the cliff. It was created in

---

How did the Valley of Rocks form?

A look at a map of the area around Lynton shows that while the Lyn (the combination of the East and West Lyn rivers) now reaches the sea at Lynmouth, it seems once to have flowed through the Valley of Rocks. As this is now dry and around 330ft (100m) above sea level, how can this be? Geologists are still debating this, but the theories about the creation of the Valley of Rocks have been reduced to two. One suggests the Ice Age created a huge ice sheet along the Bristol Channel, the ice wall creating a barrier to the Lyn's flow to the sea, forcing it to flow further west to reach open water. When the ice melted, the Lyn took a more direct route, leaving the Valley of Rocks high and dry.

The second theory proposes that the original path of the Lyn was along the Valley, but coastal erosion cut into the river near Lynmouth diverting the flow and so leaving the Valley behind. Whichever the cause, the result is a spectacular inland valley.

1817 by a local called Sanford as a result of requests, by guests at Lynton's first hotel, for a seaside walk. Some guests may have got more than they bargained for as the path makes its way above the rugged, and occasionally deeply indented, coast.

MOTHER MELDRUM – AGGIE NORMAN?

In the mid-nineteenth century Mr Norman, a local man, built a hut for his wife Aggie close to Castle Rock. From it she sold tea and snacks, but seems to have rapidly sensed the value of appearing eccentric. She therefore began to tell tales of the Doones and other local legends, while dispensing remedies based on local myths. Soon Aggie acquired a reputation as a 'white' witch and became a feature of the local tourist trade. Aggie died in 1860, just nine years before Blackmore published *Lorna Doone*. It is widely believed that Mother Meldrum who 'kept her winter in this vale of rocks, sheltering from the wind and rain within the Devil's Cheesewring' was based on Aggie.

At the lower end of the valley is **Lee Abbey**. Despite the name (and the appearance) this was never an abbey, though there was a grange farm of Forde Abbey on the Somerset-Dorset border. The present house was rebuilt in mock-Gothic style from the Wichehalse family manor house in 1841 by Charles Bailey. Later it became a hotel and then a Christian retreat and conference centre.

THE WHITE LADY

Between the Valley roundabout and Lee Abbey a signpost directs visitors to a point at which the outline of a woman is said to be visible in the profile of the hole at the top of Castle Rock. Legend has it that this is the White Lady. Exactly who the White Lady was is shrouded in mystery: some claim she is the ghost of Aggie Norman, others that she was one of the Wichehalse family who committed suicide by leaping from the cliffs of Duty Point, where there is a folly tower (now ruinous) built by the family.

The folly is occasionally called Jennifer's Leap and it said that Jennifer Wichehalse was the suicide, leaping to her death after she had been seduced by Lord Auberley during the reign of James II. It is said that Auberley promised her marriage, but having achieved his evil way dropped her. Jennifer's father complained to the king, who was a good friend of Auberley and did nothing. After Jennifer's suicide Wichehalse joined Monmouth's rebels and at Sedgemoor sought out Auberley on the field and killed him. It is a fine tale, but no corroboration exists. To make the waters even muddier, another version of the White Lady legend claims the Wichehalse suicide was called Mary…

PARRACOMBE AND WESTERN EXMOOR

Following the A39 from Barbrook the visitor climbs to Martinhoe Cross then descends towards **Parracombe**. The Normans set up a motte and bailey castle – Holwell Castle to the south of the village – and in late medieval times the village was prosperous because of its markets and an annual cattle, sheep and horse fair. Later it was a local centre for the wool trade.

Within the village be sure to look for St Petrock's, the old church – at

Churchtown, on the eastern side. When the building was declared unsafe in the nineteenth century a national fund was set up, in part by John Ruskin, for money to build a replacement elsewhere rather than demolish St Petrock's. This was done, and as a result the old church was never 'restored'. The church is twelfth/thirteenth-century, but it is the inside which draws the eye. St Petrock's is a treasure-house of interior church design from the reign of George III, with box pews, a three-decker pulpit, painted tympanum, musicians' gallery and rood screen. Elsewhere, East Bodley Farm was once owned by a member of the Blackmore family, RD Blackmore spending school holidays at the farm.

From Parracombe the A39 (which actually bypasses the village) continues south-west, exiting the National Park at **Blackmoor Gate**, named, it is believed, for the toll gate which stood here (or, perhaps, a little way south) at which farmers paid to be allowed to take their animals to graze on the 'bleak moor'.

The coast holds most of the interest in this area of the National Park, the moor itself being heavily farmed. From Barbrook a minor road does head south, through East Ilkerton, to reach access land below Ilkerton Ridge. There is one last area of excellent open walking to the south, crossing Thornworthy Common to reach a short, enigmatic stone row and the Saddle Stone boundary marker. South again is **Wood Barrow**. There is a depression in the top of this Bronze Age burial mound, a local legend claiming that it was formed when a group of locals were digging for the treasure they were sure was buried deep in the mound. At the moment they hit something, lightning struck the hole they were digging, the thunder deafening them. The lightning had struck a metal pot at the base of the hole. Very soon, a story arose that the guardians of the site had called on the lightning to evaporate the treasure that the pot had contained.

Fox and Goose Inn, Parracombe

The popular Hunters Inn

From Wood Barrow the walker should head west. There are several megalithic sites on this section of the moor: **Long Stone** is a menhir (standing stone) almost 9ft (3m) high, the tallest on Exmoor. The stone is of slate, about 3ft (a metre) wide, but quite thin. It is thought to be a marker for those approaching Longstone Barrow from the north-west. The barrow is another Bronze Age burial, and there are eleven more beyond the Long Stone, collectively called the **Chapman Barrows**. One has a trig point set on it. Close by is the **Negus Memorial** set up by Col RE Negus, Master of the Quarme Harriers to the memory of his son who died of polio aged 18.

From Martinhoe Cross the coast is regained by taking the minor road to **Martinhoe**. The area around the village has a long history, there being local evidence of Iron Age settlers: later, in about 50AD, the Romans had a signal station still called The Beacon, north-west of the village,

from which they watched the coast. The church, which has thirteenth-century origins but was much restored by the Victorians, has memorials to the Wichehalse family of Lee Abbey and also the Blackmores.

Close to Martinhoe is **Woody Bay**, which can also be reached by continuing along the minor road through the Valley of Rocks. The sheltered bay, as with Lee Bay to the east, is popular in summer. Following the coastal path (Tarka Trail or National Trail) west from Woody Bay the walker will soon reach a spectacular waterfall, a stream rising near Martinhoe dropping down the cliffs only a few hundred metres from its source.

From Martinhoe a road drops down to **Hunter's Inn** in the valley of the River Heddon. The inn is a famous tourist waymark and has been for many years. It was first a thatched inn popular with the hunters of the name but after that building had burnt down in 1895 it was rebuilt in today's more elaborate style. Close to the inn there is a National Trust shop/ice cream shop, the Trust owning land around Heddon's Mouth, which can be reached by a path that heads north from the inn.

THE TARKA TRAIL

The ancient name for a river in Devon was *Ta*, and it was also chosen by Henry Williamson as the basis of Tarka in *Tarka the Otter*. Devon County Council have waymarked a long (180 miles – 290km) trail in Tarka's honour. The route is a figure-of-eight, one circle linking Bideford, Okehampton and Barnstaple, the other Barnstaple with Lynton, with a return along the South-West Coast Path.

The Trail and the Two Moors Way long-distance path are co-incident along Cheriton Ridge as the Way nears its end-point at Lynmouth, but then the Trail branches off to follow the South-West Coast Path National Trail through the Valley of Rocks and along the coast from Woody Bay to Combe Martin. This section of the National Trail is one of the best, there being few roads that approach the coast, and even those stopping some way short, discouraging all but the most persistent of visitors. In Williamson's book, Tarka swims along the coast and rests in an old lime kiln near Heddon's Mouth (a point not actually reached by the Trails as they turn inland to cross the river).

From Hunter's Inn a minor road climbs on to Trentishoe Down. A left turn leads to the village of **Trentishoe** which has a neat fifteenth-century church. Inside, the musicians' gallery escaped the hands of the Victorian restorers. It is said that until recently a particular form of bittercress, *Cardamine trifolia*, grew in the churchyard confirming tales of local smuggling. The steep cliffs northwest of the village were deemed unclimbable, but the local men knew of a difficult, but feasible, path up them. Ships would land contraband at the foot of the cliffs and the village men would lug it up the path for hiding in the churchyard. It is assumed that seeds from the flower – which grows in France – were attached to the barrels.

AN ANCIENT CUSTOM

There is a sheaf of corn carved into the musicians' gallery of St Peter's Church, Trentishoe, a memory of an ancient local custom. The first sheaf of corn to be cut was taken to the church and then given to the youngest man in the congregation. He then took it home, attempting to shelter it from water thrown at it by fellow young men. If the sheaf stayed dry, so would the harvest, but if it was soaked, then there would be a wet harvest.

After crossing Trentishoe Down and edging past Holdstone Down, the minor road reaches Stony Corner. A right turn here follows a road that marks the border of the National Park. Northwards – but not easily reached from here, walkers must follow the Coast Path from car parks on Trentishoe Down – there is a marvellous section of coast. The road now exits the National Park and descends to Combe Martin.

Places to Visit

Devon's Exmoor

Lynton and Lynmouth Cliff Railway

Open: All year, daily 8.45am-7pm.
Open until 10pm on Bank Holidays and June-September.
☎ 01598 753486

Exmoor's Brass Rubbing and Hobbycraft Centre

Woodside Craft Centre
Watersmeet Road
Lynmouth
Open: February half-term-November daily 10.30am-5pm.
☎ 01598 752529

Lynmouth Pottery

Watersmeet Road
Lynmouth
Open: All year, daily 10am-5pm.
Often later closing June-September.
☎ 01598 752449

Glen Lyn Gorge

Lynmouth
Open: Easter-October, daily 9am-5pm. Gorge also open most days during winter.
☎ 01598 753207

Watersmeet (NT)

Nr Lynmouth
Open: Information Centre/Restaurant/Shop: April-October, daily 10.30am-5.30pm (4.30pm in October).
The valley is open all year, daily.
☎ 01598 753348

Lyn and Exmoor Museum

St Vincent's Cottage, Market Flats Lynton
Open: Easter-October, Monday-Friday 10am-12.30pm. 2-5pm, Sunday 2-5pm.
☎ 01598 752225

Horsedrawn Tours

West Ilkerton Farm
Lynton
Open: Timings vary with weather and visitor numbers.
☎ 01598 752310 for details.

4. Southern Exmoor

The northern moor – the high ground and the coast – is the famous moor, but the moorland to the south, less populated and less well-known, is equally stunning country.

DULVERTON

Dulverton, at the south-eastern tip of the National Park, is the main town of the southern moor and an excellent point from which to start exploring. Dulverton was once a cloth making town, its mills driven by the River Barle, but has always been a centre for hunting and fishing. As a field sports centre it has a very long history, Sir Robert Corun, a local man, having been prosecuted for killing a royal stag in 1365. The now controversial Devon and Somerset Staghounds was re-founded by a town resident in 1855. At one time the hunting and fishing visitors came in such numbers that there were more than 20 hotels and inns in the town, many more than can be counted today.

To explore the town, start from in front of the Visitor Centre which shares a building with the town library. The building lies at one end of Fore Street, an impressively wide main street designed to accommodate the fairs and markets that contributed to the prosperity of the town. The first fairs (two annually) were granted in 1488, but a charter of 1556 granted

Opposite page: White Horse Inn, Exford
Left: Winsford
Below: Dulverton Church

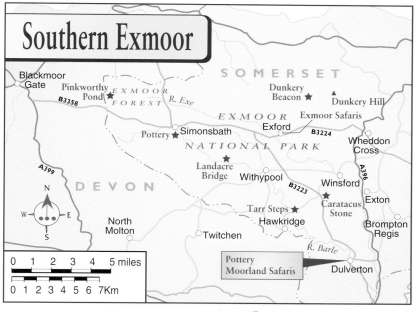

Southern Exmoor

Blackmoor
Gate
Pinkworthy   E X M O O R
Pond
B3358   F O R E S T   R. Exe

S O M E R S E T

Dunkery
Beacon ★   ▲
Dunkery Hill

E X M O O R   Exmoor Safaris
Pottery ★ Simonsbath   Exford
B3224

N A T I O N A L   P A R K   Wheddon
Cross

A399   Landacre
Bridge   Withypool
B3223   Winsford
A396

D E V O N   Caratacus
Stone ★   Exton

N   Tarr Steps ★
W ——◆—— E   Hawkridge   Brompton
S   North   Regis
Molton
Twitchen   R. Barle

0 1 2 3 4 5 miles
                    Pottery
0 1 2 3 4 5 6 7Km   Moorland Safaris   Dulverton

a Saturday market as well as confirming the fairs. Fore Street then
had a shambles (a row of butchers'
shops, not a place for the squeamish

in medieval times), a buttercross
and a market hall. Almost opposite
the library is the Town Hall, built
in the mid-nineteenth century and

incorporating the old market hall. The distinctive double steps were added in 1927 to a design by Sir Edwin Lutyens. Inside the hall there is a plaque to the 'Ten Good Men of Dulverton' who were granted the right to hold the markets and fairs. The White Hart Inn, mentioned in *Lorna Doone* (where it was praised for its 'rare and choice victuals') stood close to the Town Hall. Dulverton was also the place where Jan Ridd met Lorna.

With your back to the library, turn right and follow Fore Street around into High Street, following this to the River Barle. To the left as you walk along High Street is Chapel Lane along which lies the Laundry, once a woollen, later a silk mill, then a sawmill, but now a large laundry. Across the river, the impressive house set on the hillside was built by the Fry chocolate family of Keynsham in north Somerset. Despite its size it was called 'The Cottage'. Originally thatched, it served the family as a hunting lodge. The river is crossed by Barle Bridge, medieval in origin but widened in the early nineteenth century. From the bridge – beware of traffic – there is a fine view of the river.

Now take a path on the town side of the bridge, walking upstream to reach Exmoor House, the National Park headquarters housed in the Victorian Workhouse (hence the somewhat grim appearance), built to accommodate 52 paupers. Turn right at the house, walking through a car park and up steps to reach another car park (the Guildhall Centre car park). Between the two car parks you cross a mill leat, which once fed water to half-a-dozen wool and corn mills (including the mill that is now the laundry). The last of the mills,

the town mill (to your right), operated until 1971, powered by a waterwheel. The Guildhall now houses the Guildhall Heritage Centre that has a reconstructed cottage interior from the Dulverton of the nineteenth century and the Exmoor Photographic Archive, and also stages frequent art exhibitions.

Now continue along a narrow lane past pretty houses to return to Fore Street. Turn left and walk through Bank Square ahead to reach the town church. The tower is thirteenth century, but the rest of the building dates from the mid-nineteenth century. Inside, windows commemorate famous local men – Sir George Williams, founder of the YMCA, Gilbert Wills, Baron Dulverton, of the cigarette family, and George Peppin who emigrated to Australia in 1850 and bred the Merino sheep. The churchyard holds the grave of Thomas Chilcott.

THOMAS CHILCOTT'S TOMBSTONE

The tombstone of Thomas Chilcott who died in 1873 was once inscribed:

He was neglected by his doctor
Treated cruel by his nurse
His brother robbed his widow
Which makes it still worse

The doctor and nurse seem to have been sanguine about the libel, but the brother took Chilcott's widow to court. She was ordered to remove the words, refused and was sent to jail in Taunton. Her sentence required her to stay there until she agreed to the removal, and, eventually, she did. The space on the tombstone is now taken with the details of the wife, who died in 1881.

THE BELFRY TREE

To the west of the church is the Belfry Tree, a once vast sycamore – it overshadowed the tower – which was split by lightning in the early nineteenth century. The tree was then held together by iron bands made by the local blacksmith, probably the first example of tree surgery in the country. The tree finally succumbed, partially, to a gale in 1975. The iron bands can be seen beside the church tower.

Take the path on the right (eastern) side of the church, passing the remains of a 10ft (3m) waterwheel which once powered the smithy and continuing to reach Vicarage Hill. A detour left along the main road is worthwhile here to see 'Woodliving', a thatched, thirteenth-century cottage that served as a tannery in the sixteenth century. Return to Vicarage Hill and follow it back towards town, continuing along High Street. To the right is **Sydenham Hall** (a private house at No.45), which formed part of the dowry of Elizabeth Sydenham when she married Sir Francis Drake. To the left soon after is another car park, while to the right Union Street leads back to Fore Street.

The Sydenham family also owned the Pixton estate , the very last section of the National Park, to the south-east of the town. **Pixton Park**, the eighteenth-century mansion which now stands on the flank of Pixton Hill, was built for the Acland family and later was home to the Earls of Caernarvon one of whom famously financed the expeditions of Howard Carter which led to the discovery of Tutankhamun's tomb.

HAWKRIDGE AND TARR STEPS

To the west of Dulverton are a series of Iron Age earthworks set close to the Barle, an indication of its strategic importance. Closest to the town is **Oldbury** (or Oldberry as it is occasionally given), while further west are **Mounsey Castle** and **Brewer's Castle**, each named for a Norman lord though their construction pre-dates the Norman period by a thousand years or more.

A superb walk beside the Barle links the sites, and can be extended as far as **Hawkridge**, a tiny hamlet where anciently one of the two annual Courts of Swainmote, which regulated the behaviour of those making a living within the Forest of Exmoor, was held (the other was held at Landacre Bridge – see below). The Court was held in the churchyard. The church itself has a fine Norman font and a tradition of independently-minded clergy: one was convicted of hiding deer poachers from Devon, while another is said to have confronted the devil, defying his right to have sole use of Tarr Steps. The devil is said to have called the cloaked, presumptuous vicar a 'black crow' to which the reverend gentleman retorted that he was not as black as the devil. The verbal duel appears to have paid off as soon everyone was using the steps. The steps can be approached from Hawkridge, but are much easier to reach from the other side of the river.

To the south of Hawkridge there is good walking on the moorland of the **Anstey Commons**. There are several Bronze Age round barrows on the common together with an extraordinary memorial, a massive

Tarr Steps

granite boulder hauled here by steam lorry in 1935. The boulder – from the Barle at Dulverton – was set up to the memory of Philip Froude Hancock, a larger-than-life character who played rugby for England and hunted the moors regularly.

The easier approach to **Tarr Steps** is along a minor road that leaves the B3223 at Spire Cross a short way north-west of Dulverton. The main road leaves the town and follows the River Barle closely before breaking north and climbing through more woodland to reach open moor. From Spire Cross the road descends to a car park from where it is a short walk to the Steps. A much longer, but very fine, walk links Tarr Steps to Withypool along the eastern bank of the River Barle. The return can be made along a section of the Two Moors Way, an unofficial long distance footpath that crosses Exmoor and Dartmoor.

TARR STEPS

In 1968 the Post Office issued a set of commemorative stamps: the 4 old penny stamp (letter post) bore the image of **Tarr Steps** and the bold title 'prehistoric'. It is difficult to find a reference to the causeway before, or immediately after, that date that does not offer this view as though it were fact, but the truth is that no one knows how old Tarr Steps are. In form the Steps are a very long version of the clapper bridges more usually found on Dartmoor. In fact this is the longest clapper bridge in Britain, over 120ft (36m) long and comprising 17 spans, the biggest slab of which weighs several tons. The slabs average about 7ft (2m) long and 4ft (1.5m) wide and are held about 3ft (1m) above the water by piers placed on the stream bed.

For all its size the bridge is oddly sited: the River Barle can be successfully forded close to it for most of the year, and just a kilometre southward is another crossing known to have been in use in the mid-twelfth century. This latter fact lends weight to the argument that Tarr Steps are thirteenth- or fourteenth-century. The name, too, seems to suggest a similarity with Dartmoor – Tarr from tor, the exposed slabs of rock found on moorland summits. However, some have suggested that Tarr is from *tochar*, the Celtic word for a causeway. If the Iron Age Celts had named the bridge then a Bronze Age construction becomes more likely. Overall, the weight of evidence suggests Tarr Steps are a medieval footbridge, but with just enough doubt to maintain interest. In one sense the age of the bridge could be classified as 'recent' for severe flooding has required its rebuilding several times. The flood of 1952 that destroyed Lynmouth tore sixteen of the bridge's seventeen spans away. One stone, weighing over a ton, was moved nearly 164ft (50m) downstream. The restoration was as perfect as could be achieved and, using the best of modern equipment, difficult, merely adding to the wonder of the original construction.

One curious folk story also suggests a very early construction date. The bridge, it says, was a ritual crossing rather than a real one – the ford serving that purpose – and there was an annual animal sacrifice (usually of a cat), the poor creature being thrown across the river and killed on the far side before crossings were allowed. This legend has an echo of another Exmoor legend, suggests that the Devil built Tarr Steps so he could sunbathe near the river and that he killed any creature which crossed them. It was the Devil's slaughter of a cat that is said to have led to the confrontation between himself and the vicar of Hawkridge.

WINSFORD AND WITHYPOOL

At Spire Cross those travelling to Tarr Steps turn left: a right turn leads to Winsford, passing close to the **Caratacus Stone**. **Winsford** is a pretty village, famous as the birthplace of Ernest Bevin, trade union leader and Foreign Secretary in Atlee's post-war Labour government. He lived at the house (which bears a plaque), in the southern part of the village until he was eight. Many information sheets claim that Ernest lived here with his widowed mother, but in fact he was an illegitimate son of Diana Bevin, his father probably the local butcher. The village also has a beautiful sixteenth-century thatched hotel, once a farmhouse.

Back on the B3223 we continue north-west, passing close to the summit of Winsford Hill. From the top, on clear days, Cornwall's highest point, Brown Willy, can be seen. The sculpted land to the north is the Punchbowl: legend has it that the Devil scooped the earth to make Dunkery Beacon from here, creating the hill by throwing it over his shoulder while digging a well to satisfy his thirst after building Tarr Steps.

Further along the main road, at Comer's Cross, a right turn leads to Winsford, while a minor road on the left drops steeply down to **Withypool**, another pretty village. It is thought that under the Normans Withypool was the 'capital' of Exmoor. The Normans built a church but very little of this remains after substantial rebuilding in the fifteenth century. The fine carved font is probably original. The tower was rebuilt in 1902. It is short and squat, but this was not the architect's plan: the money ran out when the tower was this high. RD Blackmore wrote part of *Lorna Doone* in the Royal Oak Inn and Gen Dwight D Eisenhower came, by horseback it is said, for a pint after visiting American troops

The Caratacus Stone

The stone, standing in a shelter erected to protect its inscription, is carved with the words *Carataci Nepus* – kinsman of Caratacus. Caratacus led the Welsh Celts against the Romans in the first century AD, yet the inscription is fifth-or sixth-century work. It has been suggested that a later leader claimed to be a descendant of the early hero. However, the stone could be Neolithic, 2000 years earlier than the man or the carving, and the inscription faces away from the old track it stands beside – was it once erected elsewhere? As with Tarr Steps we will never know for sure.

who were training on Exmoor.

On top of Withypool Hill, to the south of the village, is one of Exmoor's very few stone circles. The circle, comprises about 40 very short stones, the tallest being barely 2ft (0.6m) high.

EXFORD AND SIMONSBATH

Back on the main road the next crossroads is at Chibbet Post. A left turn here descends to the famous **Landacre Bridge**, where the second of the two Courts of Swainmote (see Hawkridge above) was held. The fifteenth-century, five-arched bridge (also occasionally called Lanacre and Long Acre, the latter perhaps a clue to the origin of the name) is one of the moor's most famous landmarks. Beyond the bridge the minor road climbs south-eastwards, reaching the Somerset-Devon border near the Sportsman's Inn and Sandyway Cross. Here a left turn leads to **Twitchen**, a neat village, the final one within this section of the National Park. The minor road itself descends to North Molton.

At Chibbet Post a right turn leads past Court Farm, dating, in part, from the sixteenth century, where a beam is carved 'Thomas Fugars/ Anne'. This is believed to refer to the legendary Exmoor highwayman Tom Faggus (see Simonsbath below) and his wife. Beyond the farm lies **Exford**, for many the quintessential Exmoor village, the 'capital' of the moor. The village is home to the Somerset and Devon Staghounds, the hunt stables being situated on the village's western edge, close to the river. The huge green at the centre of the village was once the site of an important sheep and horse fair,

though this has not been held for over a century. There is still an annual horse show, but that is held at a separate site. On the southern side of the Green, spectacularly sited beside the Exe, is the White Horse Inn. There has been an inn on this site since at least the sixteenth century.

In the nineteenth century a stable block was added: when the village was devastated by flooding in August 1952 (a flood caused by the same storm which caused the devastation in Lynmouth) the stables were badly damaged and many loose boxes were washed away. Miraculously, none of the 23 horses at the inn were killed. Close to the inn is the picturesque Exe Bridge. There was certainly a bridge here in the 1540s when the Elizabethan traveller Leland noted a 'little tymber bridge...over the Exe brooke'.

Heading east from the Green, along Church Hill, is the village church, once dedicated to St Salvyn, a Celtic saint, but now to St Mary Magdalene. The church's rood screen was originally in the church at West Quantoxhead. It is a superb, sixteenth-century work which, astonishingly in view of its quality, lay in pieces for almost 70 years before being erected here. The churchyard has two interesting graves: Amos Cann was a young man caught in a blizzard on his way home from Porlock in March 1891 and not found for three weeks; that of Jan Glass marks the final resting place of one of the moor's most notorious sheep thieves.

At Exford, Exmoor Safari offers Landrover explorations of the high National Park.

West of Exford the B3223 passes close to Cloven Rocks where Jan

Winsford and Winsford Hill

Ridd finally met and fought Carver Doone.

THE DEATH OF
CARVER DOONE

In *Lorna Doone* John Ridd pursues Carver Doone, the villain of the story, across the moor after Carver has shot Lorna in Oare church as she is married to John. He catches him near the great black bog close to Cloven Rocks. Doone shoots Ridd, but John Ridd, a wrestling champion, is so filled with vengeance that he ignores the wound and grapples with his enemy, eventually having him in a vice-like hold. But as he calls on Doone to admit defeat, John

Ridd is horrified to see the bog, which they strayed into, sucking Carver down. 'The black bog had him by the feet; the sucking of the ground drew on him, like the thirsty lips of death...He fell back...tossed his arms to heaven...the glare of his eyes was ghastly...while, joint by joint, he sank from view.'

Just beyond Cloven Rocks is **Simonsbath**, hardly big enough to classify as a hamlet, but a notable place because of the emptiness of this area of moor. The name dates from at least the sixteenth century when it was noted by Leland. According to legend the name derives from Sigismund, a Dane who helped local Britons resist Saxon invasion. At that time there was only the name, the first house at the site being built by the London merchant (of Dutch descent) James Boevey who built Simonsbath House in 1654. Later the house was taken over by John Knight who built the village houses in the hope of developing the agricultural potential of the area, a forlorn hope as it turned out. Knight also built the church. Despite the Early English style it was actually completed in 1856.

Murder at Simonsbath

Two years after the Knights had built the church at Simonsbath there was a sensational murder in the village, William Burgess killing Anna-Maria, his 6-year old daughter and throwing her body into the shaft of Wheal Eliza, to the south. Quite why he did this is the subject of dispute. Burgess was a widower and could not afford the half-crown a week it cost to keep his daughter. However, there is another version that claims that the woman he was courting refused to marry him if she had to become mother to his daughter. The girl was missed, her body was discovered and Burgess was hanged in Taunton Jail in 1858.

A fine walk visits the remains of the Wheal Eliza mine where the body of William Burgess' daughter was thrown. Take the path opposite the pottery, going through the fine woodland of Birch Cleave (which, despite the name, is a beech wood; at 1,200ft (365m) – claimed to be the highest in England) and then follow the River Barle's bank. Wheal Eliza was begun in 1846 as a copper mine, but was never successful. Later owners tried to mine iron ore, but that venture also failed. Beyond the mine the walk can be continued to **Cow Castle**, a hill fort, probably dating from the Iron Age. North of the hill fort are the remains of Picked Stones, another mine, from where an old track heads back to Simonsbath, passing Winstitchen, once a farm of Frederic Knight, John Knight's son.

TOM FAGGUS, HIGHWAYMAN

Tom Faggus is a minor character in *Lorna Doone*, a highwayman who receives a royal pardon and becomes a respectable member of society. The highwayman of legend was a blacksmith from North Molton, who turned to crime after he lost everything – including his intended wife – in a lawsuit with a local member of the gentry. The Faggus of legend was sharp-witted and resourceful and, as is usually required of hero-villains, he was assisted by a brave and intelligent horse, Winnie, a strawberry roan. Tom and Winnie jumped off the bridge at Barnstaple to escape capture, and when cornered in an inn at Simonsbath Tom whistled for Winnie. Her stampeding gallop to him scattered his pursuers, allowing the pair to escape. On one occasion Tom robbed a gentleman, then recognised him as the man responsible for his downfall and gave him back his valuables, claiming it was not reasonable to rob a robber. It is said that Tom was eventually captured and hanged, but no record of this exists. Indeed, no record of a Tom Faggus exists at all and the carved beam at Court Farm probably refers to a member of a well-documented family from Minehead. But the legend of the gentleman outlaw lives on.

WEST FROM SIMONSBATH

From Simonsbath a minor road crosses the Barle and heads south-west, crossing both the Two Moors Way and the Tarka Trail long-distance paths. Further on, at Kinsford Gate Cross, the minor road that crosses ours, runs along the border between Somerset and Devon. To the left, this boundary road rises to **Two Barrows**, an excellent view-point. The barrows of the name – there are actually four, but two show prominently on the skyline – are Bronze Age round barrows, the largest crowned by an OS trig point. There are more barrows on Five Barrows Hill, to the right at Kinsford Gate. Here too the arithmetic is faulty, there being a total of nine round barrows, but five show on the skyline as a landmark.

Back at Simonsbath we leave the B3223, which heads north to Lynmouth, following the B3358, which runs west. About 3 miles (5km) from the village there is a car park on the right, by Goat Hill Bridge: from this a path heads north to **Pinkworthy Pond**. The pond is man-made, built on the instructions of John Knight of Simonsbath though quite why is not clear. It is possible that he intended to build a canal to service his local mines and needed a 'header tank' for it, or, perhaps, to supply water to an incline engine. The pond margins are a good place for bog plants – heath spotted orchid, bog pimpernel and the insectivorous butterwort, but many walkers prefer not to visit at dusk or at night when a strange air of malevolence seems to creep over the area.

A farmer drowned himself in the pond in 1889 leaving his coat and hat neatly on the bank. Attempts to find his body by dragging and diving failed – there was even one attempt based on an old tale that a candle floated on a loaf of bread would automatically float to a point directly above the body, but that technique failed too – and eventually the pond was drained and the body found. In 1913 the pond was drained again, but this time the body of a supposed suicide was not discovered. From the pond, The Chains, one of the last areas of 'old' Exmoor can be reached. Though bogs of the type that swallowed Carver Doone are now a memory, The Chains are still part of a wild, weather-swept landscape.

Continuing west along the B3358, a left turn leads through the scattered, but pretty, hamlet of **Challacombe** – the name means 'cold valley' an indication of the exposure and remoteness of the site – and out of the National Park. Close to where the road reaches the A399 is the **Exmoor Steam Railway**, a miniature, narrow-gauge railway running on a 2 mile (3km) track. There is also a children's play area and a model railway. Now turn right along the A399, then left to reach South Stowford and the **Exmoor Zoo**, which has over 150 species (mostly smaller animals and birds) on a large site. There is a children's playground and a good café.

Places to Visit

Southern Exmoor

Guildhall Heritage Centre

Monmouth Terrace
Dulverton
Open: One week before Easter-
October, daily 10am-4.30pm.
☎ 01398 324081

Exmoor Safaris

Exford
Open: Morning, afternoon and
evening trips, timings dependent on
weather and visitor numbers.
☎ 01643 831229/831112

Exmoor Steam Railway

Cape of Good Hope Farm
Nr Bratton Fleming
Open: mid-March-April Wednesday
and Sunday 10.30am-5pm, but open
all over Easter; May Tuesday,
Wednesday and Sunday 10.30am-
5pm, but also open May Day and
Whitsun; June-mid-July Tuesday-
Thursday and Sunday 10.30am-5pm;
mid-July-August, daily 10.30am-
5pm; September Tuesday-Thursday
and Sunday 10.30am-5pm; October
Tuesday, Wednesday and Sunday
10.30am-5pm. *Also open for Santa
special on weekends close to
Christmas, telephone for details.*
☎ 01598 710711

Exmoor Zoo

South Stowford
Open: All year, daily 10am-6pm (4pm
from October-March).
☎ 01598 763352

5. North Devon

In this chapter, we visit the country to the west of the National Park, following the North Devon coast to Morte Point, then turning south to reach Barnstaple before returning cross-country to reach the National Park again.

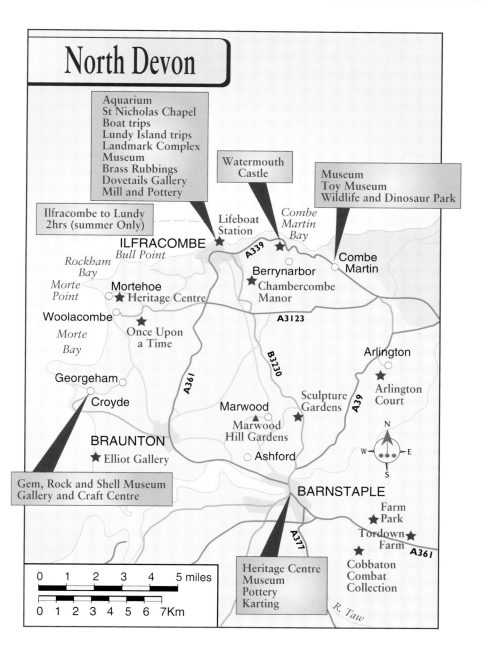

North Devon

Aquarium
St Nicholas Chapel
Boat trips
Lundy Island trips
Landmark Complex
Museum
Brass Rubbings
Dovetails Gallery
Mill and Pottery

Watermouth
Castle

Museum
Toy Museum
Wildlife and Dinosaur Park

Ilfracombe to Lundy
2hrs (summer Only)

Lifeboat
Station

*Combe
Martin
Bay*

ILFRACOMBE

*Rockham
Bay*

Bull Point

Berrynarbor

*Combe
Martin*

*Morte
Point*

Mortehoe
★ Heritage Centre

Chambercombe
Manor

Woolacombe

Once Upon
a Time

A3123

*Morte
Bay*

B3230

Arlington

Georgeham

A361

Marwood

Sculpture
Gardens

Arlington
Court

Croyde

Marwood
Hill Gardens

A39

N
W — E
S

BRAUNTON
★ Elliot Gallery

Ashford

Gem, Rock and Shell Museum
Gallery and Craft Centre

BARNSTAPLE

Farm
★ Park

Tordown
Farm

A361

A371

Cobbaton
Combat
Collection

Heritage Centre
Museum
Pottery
Karting

R. Taw

0	1	2	3	4	5 miles

0	1	2	3	4	5	6	7Km

COMBE MARTIN AND WATERMOUTH

Combe Martin derives its name from the valley along which it straggles and the Martin family who were twelfth-century landowners. From the thirteenth century, perhaps earlier, the town's prosperity was based on mining, silver and later iron and umber. Mining lasted, with varying levels of activity, until the early 1900s, a period of not less than 600 years. All that now remains is a collection of ruins and some adits and shafts, the latter best avoided – though as virtually all the mines lie on private land they are, in any case, off-limits. The clearest reminder of the mining is the ruins of the engine house of a silver mine on Knap Down, to the east of the town. The ruins, standing on land of the aptly named Silver Mines Farm, can be viewed from nearby footpaths, but should not be approached.

The Last Martin

Legend states that the Martins had a moated castle or lodge at Combe Martin from which they hunted regularly on west Exmoor. One day Robert, the last of the Martin line, went out hunting early one morning. When he had not returned at nightfall, the drawbridge across the moat was raised, the servants thinking that Robert had decided to stay elsewhere. When he finally returned in the dead of night the weary hunter failed to spot the raised drawbridge, rode his horse into the moat and was drowned. It is said that a knight on a white horse still haunts the site of the long-gone lodge, at the southern end of the town.

Combe Martin consists of little more than one long street, which makes it very picturesque when approached along the A399, but tedious for exploring. As the main sites lie between the church and the sea, we still start from the latter.

The beach is well-sheltered and offers exciting walks/scrambles along the rocks of its eastern side, towards Lester Point. On the other side, a path from Seaside Hill leads to **Newberry Beach**. There are well-worn steps cut into the rocks beyond the beach, named Phoenician Steps from the dubious story that they were cut to service the boats of Phoenician traders buying local silver. The **museum**, above the beach, explores the history of the village, with sections on mining and the burning of lime in local kilns for agricultural use.

Nearby, the Wonder Years Toy Museum has a collection spanning the years from 1950-1990.

The main street starts out as Borough Road then becomes King Street: continue along this to reach the **Pack o' Cards**, on the right. The house was built in about 1690 by George Ley, a noted local benefactor. According to local tradition Ley obtained the money for the house by winning at cards and to celebrate designed a house with 52 windows and 52 stairs, and with four floors on each of which there are 13 doors. Some of the windows were later bricked up, probably after the introduction of the Window Tax. Beside the house is the old Town Hall.

The Combe Martin Fire Brigade

In 1930 the Town Council was meeting one evening, the first item on the agenda being the creation of a Combe Martin Fire Brigade. The Town Hall was at that time mainly used as the local magistrates' court and for social events and so the Council was being held in another building. As the debate progressed, someone burst in to report that the Town Hall was on fire. Believing the messenger to be a practical joker the Council ignored him – and the Town Hall was gutted.

King Street becomes High Street, and the visitor passes to the left, **Reubendale House and Corelli's**. Marie Corelli was a late nineteenth/early twentieth-century writer, very popular at the time, but almost unknown today. She wrote one of her most famous novels – one which made her very rich – at the Pack o' Cards in the 1890s. Called *The Mighty Atom*, the book's central character, Reuben Dale, was based on Combe Martin's sexton. The houses commemorate the book and author.

Further on again, High Street becomes Church Street at what was once High Cross where markets and fairs were held. To the right here is the **Church of St Peter ad Vincula** (St Peter in Chains). The church tower, about 100ft (30m) high, is one of the finest in the area. It was built in the late twelfth/early fourteenth century, some of the fabric of the remaining church being 100 years older. Inside there is a magnificent fifteenth-century carved oak

screen, the rood dating from 1962, being the work of Colin Shearing in apple wood.

Finally, and the visitor should drive, it being too far to walk, further along the village street/main road is the **Wildlife and Dinosaur Park**. Here there is a collection of 250 species of animals, including snow leopards, meerkats and otters; regular displays of falconry; a dinosaur museum of fossils and skeletons; life-size dinosaurs, including animated velociraptors; and some exotic features too. Chief of these are the chance to swim with sea lions and an earthquake train ride. The site has a hotel, cafeteria and picnic area.

Westwards from Combe Martin the A399 heads inland at first, before turning north to reach Watermouth Bay. Before the Bay, turns to the left reach **Berrynarbor** and the Sterridge Valley. Berrynarbor is an attractive village set on the steep sides of the valley. The curious name derives from Berry de Narbert a Norman Lord of the Manor. The church has a splendid fifteenth-century tower and interesting seventeenth-century murals. The Sterridge Valley to the south of Berrynarbor is very attractive, but has few opportunities for walkers.

BERRYNARBOR CHURCH

In a local rhyme, the church here is compared to those of nearby Combe Martin, and with Hartland further to the south:

> *Hartland for length*
> Berrynarbor for strength
> *Combe Martin for beauty*

Watermouth Castle, close to the deeply-indented Watermouth Bay, was built in the 1825, possibly on the foundations of a much older, true castle. Today it is a family theme park with an impressive list of attractions, including model railway, doll collection, dungeons with all manner of ghosts and ghouls, and play areas/rides by the dozen. The price is all inclusive, apart from food and drink which can be bought from several cafés/snack bars.

ILFRACOMBE

West of Watermouth the visitor soon reaches **Ilfracombe**, which began life as a fishing and trading port. It is first mentioned during the early thirteenth century and was granted a market and a fair in 1278. The town was clearly prosperous: it provided ships for Edward II's campaign against Robert Bruce, and also for the siege of Calais in 1346. As a trading and fishing port the town was always busy, but real prosperity arrived with the first influx of tourists during the Napoleonic wars, when the French Riviera became out-of-bounds to the English nobility. During the latter half of the nineteenth century the holiday trade increased dramatically, many of the grand buildings beside the harbour being built at this time. The harbour is still a focal point of the town, though the demands of the modern holidaymaker mean that the attractions of Ilfracombe's have expanded away from the Victorian resort's heart. From the harbour boats leave for Lundy Island, and also for cruises along the Exmoor coast and across to South Wales. One of the regular cruise ships is the *Waverley*, the world's only sea-going paddle steamer.

Lantern Hill, on the seaward side of the harbour, is named for the red lantern that has warned shipping of rocks below since medieval times. The light shines from the small tower of St Nicholas' Chapel, built in the fourteenth century. St Nicholas is the patron saint of sailors. The chapel became a private house in the early nineteenth century but was then abandoned. It was restored in 1962 by the Ilfracombe Rotary Club and is now open to the public: there are fine views from the hill.

Beneath the chapel is Ilfracombe's Aquarium, which explores the life in an Exmoor river from its source to the sea and then explores coastal sea life. There is also a section on Lundy's Marine Reserve.

As the south-western corner of the harbour is the town's **Lifeboat Station**. The boat can be viewed, and wall charts tell of past rescues and the work of the service.

Along the coast from Lantern Hill is **Capstone**, criss-crossed by paths so that visitors can enjoy the views from its top. The huge mass of Capstone offers shelter to some of the entertainments on what would otherwise be the sea front. There is a small beach at Wildersmouth, beside Capstone, then the unmistakable, extraordinary **Landmark** complex. The truncated cones were the design of Tim Ronalds and were voted one of the ten most significant buildings in the 1990s. The cones house a theatre and a pavilion, the latter home to numerous functions. The Ilfracombe Tourist Information Office is also found here. Beside the Landmark is a beautiful, and peaceful garden in which stands the **town museum** with a remarkably eclectic collection. The Lundy Room is devoted to material on the island. The museum also offers visitors the chance to complete rubbings on facsimile brasses.

Above: Ilfracombe harbour Below: The gardens at Arlington Court

West of the Landmark is **Tunnel's Beach**, reached through a man-made tunnel behind the Palm Court Hotel, which is sheltered by spectacular cliffs, and, further on, White Pebble Beach above which winds the **Torrs Walk**, popular with generations of visitors for its views of the rugged coast. Walkers will also enjoy **Cairn Top**, a wooded nature reserve at the south-western end of the town – follow the A36 (St Brannocks Road), entrance from Ilfracombe also has beaches on the other side of the harbour – Larkstone Beach and **Rapparee Cove**, the latter surrounded by tall, steep cliffs. Further east is **Hele Bay**, another popular beach. Here the **Old Corn Mill** is a sixteenth-century watermill powered by an 18ft overshot wheel. The mill can be visited – it is still in use: flour can be purchased – both to see the machinery and the pottery, which is made on the premises by Robin Gray. Also available are tearooms and a teagarden.

Above the 'seaside' resort of Ilfracombe – Wilder Road and the harbour – is the 'modern' town. High Street is the main shopping street, though the side streets are also worth a look. At its western end, High Street becomes Church Street, leading to **Holy Trinity Church**. There was a Saxon church here, then an early Norman foundation, which was extended in the thirteenth century. Holy Trinity is claimed to have the finest waggon-roof in the West County, a fifteenth-century marvel of carved basses and figures.

Finally, two sites close to Ilfracombe are worth visiting. To the south-east of the town – take the B3230 – is **Chambercombe Manor**, an eleventh-century manor house with rooms furnished in different period styles from Elizabethan to Victorian. The house is surrounded by four acres of gardens that include a small arboretum. There are tea rooms serving light lunches. Of more interest to younger visitors will be **Keypitts**, where quad bikes can be driven off-road: follow Marlborough Road (the Old Barnstaple Road) southwards from the western end of Church street.

LUNDY

Lundy, which dominates the horizon for visitors looking west from Morte Point, is 3 miles (5km) long and just over $1/2$ mile (1km) at its widest, a lump of granite set off the north Devon coast. It is said that St Patrick, who famously rid Ireland of

The Ilfracombe Lady Redcoats

It is said that on 22 February 1797 four French ships sailed into view off Ilfracombe. With most of the local menfolk away, this being the time of the Napoleonic Wars, the town – and, indeed, the country – looked vulnerable. The town's women therefore removed their traditional red petticoats, wrapped them around their shoulders and took up prominent positions on the cliffs. The French commander, fearing that the town was protected by a large group of redcoats, fled. It is a lovely tale. But it is also told at several other places elsewhere in Britain and its provenance is dubious so......

snakes, performed the same task on Lundy. The island is fertile and surrounded by good fishing and so has been long inhabited, but its isolation has meant that the residents did not always have a peaceful time with visits from the Vikings and pirates. The thirteenth-century, ruined castle was built by Henry III with money raised by the sale of rabbits, the island having been a Royal warren at the time.

The Old Light on the plateau dates from 1819, but as it was frequently obscured by fog it was replaced by the north and south lighthouses, which were built lower down the cliffs in 1896. A fog gun battery on the west side is still *in situ* and is a fascinating place to observe sea birds and the interaction of waves and rocks. Both lighthouses are now automatic.

Lundy should never be referred to as Lundy island. Lundy is Norse for 'puffin island'. The 'y' is the same suffix as is found in Guernsey, Alderney, Orkney, Anglesey, and so on.

Today Lundy is owned by the National Trust and has a handful of full-time residents who farm and raise sheep and cattle. In spring and summer the population is boosted by tourists – bird watchers and rock climbers making for the cliffs, which rise to 400ft (130m) and those looking for time away from the mainland's hustle and bustle. Over 30 bird species nest here, but almost 300 different species have been recorded. The island is also famous for its animal life, with Soay sheep, sika deer and Lundy ponies on land and basking sharks and dolphins in the surrounding sea. **Climbers should note that restrictions apply to certain cliffs during the nesting season.**

THE SKELETON ON THE BED

When, in 1865, a tenant of Chambercombe Manor was carrying out some repairs he noticed that there was a disparity between internal and external dimensions of a room. In a small, sealed room he found an old bedstead on which was the skeleton of a woman. Legend has it that she was a wealthy lady rescued from a shipwreck, who was either robbed and entombed alive or died of her injuries and was robbed after. But in either case why wall her up rather than bury her in the park? Another story suggests she was a daughter of the owner of the manor at the time, but suggests no reason for the crime. Of course, there are those who reckon that the whole tale is a myth.

LEE BAY TO WOOLACOMBE

The main road from Ilfracombe, the A361, heads south for Braunton, but we take the B3231, turning right off the main road, to explore Devon's north-west corner. A minor road on the right, beyond Higher Slade, leads to **Lee**, a charming village at the back of Lee Bay. The picturesque houses, including *The Grampus*, a fourteenth-century inn, Smugglers' Cottage, which dates from the sixteenth century, and the delightful Old Maids' Cottage, are set in Fuchsia Valley, so-called because of the profusion of fuchsias.

THE THREE OLD MAIDS OF LEE

The story of the old maids is a local legend and inspired a poem by FE Weatherby in 1883. The three were young ladies of the village who 'were fair as fair can be' and 'they had lovers three by three' but were so fastidious in their choice of husband that they always found something wrong the suitors:

These young maids they cannot find
A lover each to suit her mind
The plain-spoke lad is far too rough
The rich young lord is not rich enough

In the end the three grow old and end as spinsters that no one wants to marry:

There are three old maids at Lee
And one is deaf, and one cannot see
They are as old as old can be
And they are all cross as a gallows tree
These three old maids of Lee

From Lee walkers can reach **Bull Point,** which has a lighthouse to warn of the point and nearby Morte Point, but drivers must make for **Mortehoe.** The church here, originally built by the Normans has an altar tomb to Sir William de Tracey. Some experts believe him to be the builder of the church, claiming a date of 1322 for his death, but a local legend claims he was one of the murderers of Thomas à Becket. From the village a straightforward walk visits Morte Point for views to Lundy Island and along the coast to Bull Point to the north, and Woolacombe Sands and Baggy Point to the south. The **Heritage Centre,** housed in a Grade II listed barn beside the play area at the village car park, explores the history of Mortehoe and the area.

South of Mortehoe is **Woolacombe,** an Edwardian resort built to take advantage of the 1½ mile (2.5km) sandy beach which backs Morte Bay between the village and Baggy Point. Because it faces west, the beach is

The Wrecks of Morte Stone

Morte Stone, off Morte Point, was given its name by the Normans, the English version of Death Stone being appropriate for so notorious a ship wrecker. In the days of sail, ships attempting to run the weather around Morte Point often finished on the stone. In the winter of 1852, five ships were lost, the death toll spurring the authorities into action, though it was not until 1879 that the lighthouse on Bull Point was finally operational. A local legend has it that any man who can control his wife can also lift and move Morte Stone. Visitors can draw their own conclusions from the fact that the stone is still in place.

free of the mud which can sometimes be found on the north coast beaches from silt-carry of the River Severn, and also occasionally experience great breakers from the Atlantic which makes it a favourite with surfers. The dunes that back the beach are owned by the National Trust and are an ecologically important site for dune plants such as sea holly and restharrow.

To head south from Woolacombe it is possible to take a steep, narrow road which climbs the flank of Woolacombe Down, but it is better to take the B3343 to Turnpike Cross. Close to this **Once Upon a Time** is a children's theme park with a variety of entertainments and rides. The park is a sister to Watermouth Castle, sharing the same philosophy of 'pay at the door,

Henry Williamson and Tarka the Otter

Henry Williamson settled in Georgeham after his return from the World War I. There he wrote a book dealing with the life and death of an otter among the otter hunts in the Land of the Two Rivers (the Taw and the Torridge). The book, *Tarka the Otter*, won the Hawthornden Prize in 1928. Though Williamson lived to the north of the Torridge it was that river that he loved. He had his animal-hero born in a holt near the canal bridge on the river between Weare Gifford and Landcross, two hamlets about 2 miles (3km) apart, Weare Gifford being about 3 miles (5km) down river from Great Torrington. At the end of the book the waters of Torridge close over the heads of Tarka and Deadlock the otter-hound as they fight their last battle close to Landcross. In later life Williamson moved to Norfolk, but when he died in 1977 he was buried at Georgeham.

then nothing more', except for food and drink (and also for one specific ride).

A right turn at Turnpike Cross follows the B3231 south. Despite the B classification this is a narrow road, and as it is often busy in summer can be a test of driving skill and patience. The road is easier after **Georgeham**, an attractive village of thatched and slate-roofed cottages. Soon after the 1914-18 War, Henry Williamson came to Georgeham, renting Skirr Cottage at first. In 1928 he bought Ox's Cross on the hill above the village for £125, £100 of it the prize money for the Hawthornden Prize. Williamson is buried in the churchyard of St George's Church.

CROYDE AND BRAUNTON

Beyond Georgeham is **Croyde**, another picturesque village of thatched cottages. It is claimed the village is named for a Viking raider, Crydda, who came in pre-Saxon times.

In the main street, the **Gem, Rock and Shell Museum** is worth a visit for its collection of stones, both local and from much further afield, and its displays of jewellery. Also worth visiting is the **Chapel Farm Gallery and Craft Centre**. The farm dates from the seventeenth century, the chapel from three centuries earlier. Originally the two formed part of St Helen's Priory. The gallery exhibits and sells the work of local artists and craftsmen.

The headlands of Saunton Down and Baggy Point enclose, pincer-like, Croyde Bay, which is almost as long as it is wide. This trick of local geography stacks water up into the bay's mouth, the length of the beach-line, allowing wave patterns to develop. As a result, any reasonable day will see surfers and canoeists in droves riding the high, long waves into the Bay. At the Bay's back is the village of Croyde Bay, a pure holiday resort.

To the north-west of Croyde Bay, reached by a walk from a National Trust car park is **Baggy Point** a headland that is part of the Devonian/ Old Red Sandstone rock belt that sweeps across North Devon below

Exmoor. The area is a favourite haunt of rock climbers, the steep faces and sweeping slabs drawing them magnetically. **During the seabird nesting season climbers are restricted to certain areas of the cliffs only.** Birds that breed regularly here include several species of gull, fulmars, shags and cormorants. Gannets are often seen, while the 'inland' cliff area is a favourite with skylarks.

BAGGY LEAP

The rock ridge going north-west from Baggy Point is Baggy Leap on which, in 1799, HMS *Weazle* was wrecked, her crew of 106 dying in one of Devon's most appalling disasters. The white pole on the cliff near the point is a coastguard training mast where exercises with rescue rocks and breeches buoys take place. Only when you gaze down at the rocks and think about the *Weazle* do you realise that such exercises are not games.

From Croyde the B3231 rounds Saunton Down, with excellent coastal views, then goes through Saunton to reach **Braunton**. Here the **museum** explores the history of the village, but one important site lies just out-side the village, to the south. **Great Field** is one of only two Saxon strip-farms left in England and is still in use. The site is crossed by a public footpath. Great Field lies inland from **Braunton Burrows**, a very important conservation area.

Back in the village be sure to visit the **church**, a thirteenth-century building with a crooked, lead-shingled spire, some excellent carvings – look particularly for the sixteenth-century bench ends – and memorials. The church is dedicated to St Brannock, a Celtic missionary who crossed the Bristol Channel from South Wales. In a dream Brannoc was told to build a church where he first saw a sow and piglets, a meeting commemorated in a carved roof boss above the north door. Also worth visiting is the **Elliot Gallery** in Hillsview that exhibits the work of contemporary artists and craftworkers.

From Braunton, take the A361 eastwards to reach **Ashford Gardens** at the left turn to Ashford. The gardens cover two acres, landscaped around a lake stacked with koi carp. There is also a butterfly house where tropical butterflies fly free in a jungle habitat. The complete life cycle of the insects can be followed

Braunton Burrows

Braunton Burrows is a National Nature Reserve set up to protect a remarkably varied number of habitats, woodland, open scrub, and wet and dry dunes, as well as the beach of Saunton Sands. The reserve is chiefly of interest for its plant life which includes many unusual species. The woodland has oak, ash, beech and willow, the trees supporting a number of rare lichens. The open scrub supports viper's bugloss and sea buckthorn, while the wet dunes have pyramidal orchid, marsh helleborine, and bird's foot trefoil. The drier dunes support sea spurge, on which the rare spurge hawk moth feeds, as well as marram grass, which, of course, binds the sand and so maintains the dunes. The beach margin plants include sea rocket, sea beet and sea couch together with prickly softwort.

in the house.

Now go through Ashford to reach Marwood and the **Marwood Hill Gardens**, a quite remarkable private garden developed over 30 years of loving care. In early spring the snow-drops and daffodils are beautiful. Later the camellias and magnolias add their colour, rhododendrons taking over in summer. There are herbaceous and alpine borders, and three lakes are linked to create the biggest bog garden in the West Country. An old walled garden has been converted into a nursery for plant sales.

BARNSTAPLE

Continuing along the A361 the visitor soon reaches **Barnstaple**, one of the highlights of north Devon, a town which is at once both histori-cally interesting and extremely at-tractive even if the one-way system can seem nightmarish to the first-time visitor. Barnstaple has a claim to being the oldest borough in En-gland, having a charter from 930, granted by Athelstan. Borough sta-tus allowed Barnstaple to mint its own coins, and some from the reign of Eadwig (955-959) remain. When the Normans came they constructed a motte, an artificial mound, for a castle: the mound can still be seen, to the north of the old railway sta-tion – on its summit are the remains of a stone keep.

The town's position on the navi-gable Taw, ensured it became an important port, especially during the early medieval period when the De-von wool trade flourished. After an eventful Civil War, when it changed hands four times, the town became an important shipbuilding centre as well as a port. Though both declined

because of silting of the Taw the town, the largest in North Devon, is still a thriving, bustling place – its three-day annual fair in September (starting at noon on the Wednesday preceding the 20th) draws large crowds – and an ideal centre for exploring the area covered by this book, as well as that to the south.

A tour of Barnstaple is best started from **Queen Anne's Walk** beside the river. The building was originally built in 1609 as a merchant's ex-change, but was rebuilt in 1708. The statue of Queen Anne tops the build-ing, a tribute to her assistance in the providing cash for the work. With its arcades it is a fine building: the Tome Stone beneath the Queen's statue was used by merchants to finalise bargains. After a deal had been struck verbally the agreed price was placed on the stone. Queen Anne's Walk now houses the **Heritage Centre,** which explores Barnstaple's history with a series of audio-visual displays.

From the centre walk to the river. As you face it, the old shipbuilding centre and main quay are to your right. To your left is **Long Bridge.**

The Maiden Arches

The three arches of Long Bridge on the town side are called the Maiden Arches because, legend has it, the money for them was provided by three wealthy spinsters. Historians believe it is more likely that the name is a corruption of midden arches because they were used by the townsfolk to throw rubbish into the Taw, a much less romantic idea.

The first bridge here is recorded in about 1280. That was of stone and is the basis of what we see today. That earliest bridge was for packhorses and pedestrians and had a chapel at the town end. It was about 9ft (3m) wide and has now been widened three but its original character was maintained each time. On the far side of the bridge is the town's leisure centre.

Now walk along the riverbank to reach **Bridge Chambers**, built in the 1870s in neo-Gothic style. Go under Long Bridge to reach the **Museum of Barnstaple and North Devon**. This building also dates from the 1870s and was the original town library and museum. The museum explores the history and natural history of north Devon, the collection including Barnstaple-minted Saxon coins and such curios as a giant leatherback turtle. There are also collections on Devon's regiments and RAF Chivenor, a World War II airfield.

A detour now crosses the eastern edge of The Square. The **Albert Memorial Clock** was built in memory of Prince Albert, Queen Victoria's husband: the four clock faces are notorious for showing different times. Turn right along Litchdon Street to reach, to the left, the **Old Brannam Pottery** (Nos. 10 and 11) with a facade of coloured brick and terracotta. One of the bottle-shaped kilns has been retained. The site is now a showroom, the pottery having moved to the Roundswell Industrial Estate. A little further on, and also on the left, are the exquisite **Penrose Almshouses** built in 1627 with money left by John Penrose, a wealthy cloth merchant who died in 1620. The almshouses were for twenty poor couples.

Return to The Square, crossing it and bearing right into Boutport Street, then left into High Street. There are excellent buildings here, some dating from the early seventeenth century (the Three Tuns Inn at the far end may even be sixteenth century), others from Victorian times. No 97, to the left, dates from about 1700: look for the faces on the keystones.

Turn right along Church Lane. There are two sets of **almshouses** here, built with endowments from Thomas Horwood and Gilbert Paige, both early seventeenth-century merchants. The buildings set off this most delightful part of the town – it

John Gay and The Beggar's Opera

John Gay, poet and playwright, was born on the corner of Joy Street and High Street in 1685. His most famous work, *The Beggar's Opera*, was a satire on contemporary political life and the pretensions of grand opera. Though condemned by the Archbishop of Canterbury and other members of the Establishment for its portrayal of London's low-life, the opera was extremely popular with ordinary folk. The opera was the inspiration for Bertolt Brecht's *Threepenny Opera*. Gay died in 1732 and is buried in Westminster Abbey's Poets' Corner. Gay wrote his own epitaph – 'Life is a jest and all things show it, I thought so once and now I know it'.

is called the churchyard – with its narrow, pedestrianised alleys. Another benefaction of the Horwood's is **Alice Horwood's School**, also in Church Lane. Alice was Thomas' wife. The school was for 'twenty poor maids, for ever' but closed, as a school, in 1814. Interestingly, the girls were taught to read, but not to write.

St Peter's Church, in Paternoster Row at the end of Church Lane dates, in part, from the early twelfth century, but was rebuilt two hundred years later. The famous, twisted, lead-clad spire was added to the tower in 1632. The second religious building in the churchyard, opposite the church, is **St Anne's Chapel**. This ancient chapel was converted to the grammar school in the sixteenth century and remained the school until 1910. John Gay was a pupil here.

Going between the church and chapel the visitor reaches **Butchers' Row**. The Row and the **Pannier Market** opposite were built in 1855, a remarkable example of Victorian town planning. The Row comprised about 30 butcher shops, while the market was for fruit and vegetables. The shops are no longer exclusively butchers and the market now sells a wider range of goods. Market day is Friday. A right turn along Butchers' Row leads to the Tourist Information Centre, while a left turn leads to High Street. Turn left, then right along Cross Street to return to Queen Anne's Walk.

Elsewhere in town, **Brannam's Pottery** on the Roundswell Industrial Estate, south of the Taw, is worth a visit. Brannam's most famous range, Royal Barum Ware – Barum was the Roman name for Barnstaple – in red and blue glaze is made here from local clay. Visitors can tour the factory, enjoy the museum or try their hand at throwing a pot.

AROUND BARNSTAPLE

Younger visitors will enjoy the **North Devon Karting Centre** on the Pottington Business Park (on the southern side of the A361 to the west of the town). There are two tracks, a shorter one for novices and younger children and a longer one for the more adventurous. Younger visitors may also enjoy a detour along the A361 to the **North Devon Farm Park**, between Landkey and Swimbridge, where there is a pets' corner, unusual farm animals, including rare pigs and sika deer, and tractor, cart and pony rides. There is also a play area and a café. Close by, **Tordown Farm** has interesting farm breeds including Red Rubies, traditional North Devon cattle.

Also close to the A361 the **Cobbaton Combat Collection** is an array of militaria from the wars of the last half of the 20th century.

From Barnstaple the A39 heads north. Beyond the hospital, turn left on the B3230 to reach **Broomhill**, a small Victorian hotel. Here the grounds are a sculpture garden of contemporary work by artists from all over Europe. There is also an art gallery. Back on the A39 the visitor soon reaches a right turn for **Shirwell**, where Sir Francis Chichester is buried. Sir Francis' father was rector of the village church and he spent much of his early life here. The Chichesters were related to Rosalie Chichester (Rosalie was Sir Francis' aunt) who is associated with **Arlington Court** a little further north along the A39. The family owned the estate for over 500 years, but the present building dates from the early nineteenth century. Inside it is crammed with treasures and curios collected by Rosalie Chichester, an inveterate traveller. Of particular interest is the collection of carriages: carriage rides in the park are possible, as are carriage driving courses. The Court is surrounded by 27 acres (11 hectares) of lovely grounds which are explored by a series of waymarked walks.

SIR FRANCIS CHICHESTER

Francis Charles Chichester was born in 1901 and after being educated in England emigrated to New Zealand where he worked as a property developer and learned to fly. When he returned to Britain he bought a Gypsy Moth aeroplane which he flew solo to Australia in 1929. He then flew solo across the Tasman Sea from east to west, a marvellous feat of navigation. He later set up a publishing company in Britain. He took up ocean racing in the 1950s and after he had overcome lung cancer in 1958/59 he won the inaugural Trans-Atlantic single-handed race in 1960. He came second in the race in 1962. In 1967 he sailed solo around the world, stopping only once in Sydney. He was knighted with Sir Francis Drake's sword on his return. He died in 1972.

Beyond Arlington Court the A39 reaches Blackmoor Gate and the border of the Exmoor National Park.

Places to Visit

North Devon

Town Museum

4 Kingsley Terrace
Combe Martin
Open: Late May-mid-September, Sunday-Friday 1.30-3.30pm. Open 11am-3.30pm during school summer holidays, and Sundays from mid-April-late May. ☎ 01271 882636

Wonder Years Toy Museum

Combe Martin
Open: April-October daily 10.30am-5pm. ☎ 01271 889277

Wildlife and Dinosaur Park

Combe Martin
Open: mid-March-October, daily 10am-3pm (last entry)
☎ 01271 882486

Watermouth Castle

Watermouth Bay, between Combe Martin and Ilfracombe
Open: mid-July-August, Sunday-Friday 10am-7pm (last ride at 6pm); April-mid-July, September and October, Sunday-Friday 11am-6pm (last ride at 5pm). ☎ 01271 867474

St Nicholas Chapel

Lantern Hill
Ilfracombe
Open: Easter and May-October, daily 10am-12noon, 2-5pm. Also open 6-9pm June-August.

Boat Trips

Ilfracombe Coastal Cruises
9 The Quay
Timetable and tickets available at Tourist Information Centre, Landmark Complex or Tel: 01271 879727

Waverley and Balmoral steamers
Brochures and timetables available
from Tourist Information Centre,
Landmark Complex (☎ 01271
863001) or ☎ 0141 2432224

Lundy Island cruises
Brochures and timetables available
from Tourist Information Centre,
Landmark Complex (☎ 01271
863001) or ☎ 01237 863001

Landmark Complex

Wilder Road
Ilfracombe
Open: Various times depending on
shows, functions etc. Tourist
Information office open daily in
summer, Monday-Saturday in winter.
☎ 01271 324242 (booking office and
What's On)
01271 865655 (theatre and to
arrange a tour of the complex)
01271 863001 (Tourist Information
Office)

Town Museum and Brass Rubbing Centre

Wilder Road
Ilfracombe
Open: April-October, daily 10am-
5pm; November-March, Monday-
Friday 10am-1pm. ☎ 01271 863541

Aquarium

Nr Harbour, Ilfracombe
Open: mid-February-October daily
10am-4.30pm (6pm in July and
August), November-January daily
10am-3pm. ☎ 01271 864533

Dovetails Gallery

60 High Street
Ilfracombe
Open: All year, Monday-Wednesday
and Friday 9am-5pm.
☎ 01271 864769

Old Corn Mill and Pottery

Hele Bay
Ilfracombe
Open: April-October, daily except

Sunday, 10am-5pm, (6pm in August:
also open Sunday in August). At
other times by request.
☎ 01271 863185

Chambercombe Manor

Ilfracombe
Open: Easter-October, Monday-
Friday 10.30am-5.30pm, Sunday 2-
5.30pm. ☎ 01271 862624

Keypitts Stables 'n' Quads

Ilfracombe
Open: Easter-October, daily 10am-
5pm, November-Easter by
appointment. ☎ 01271 862247

Heritage Centre

Mortehoe
Open: Easter-October Sunday-
Thursday 10am-3pm. Open every day
10am-6pm during school summer
holidays and 10am-5pm at Bank
Holiday weekends. ☎ 01271 870028

Once Upon a Time

On B3343 near Woolacombe
Open: mid-July-August, Sunday-
Friday 10.30am-4pm (last
admission); April-mid-July and
September, Sunday-Friday 11am-
4pm (last admission).
☎ 01271 870900

Gem, Rock and Shell Museum

10 Hobbs Hill
Croyde
Open: Easter-September, daily 10am-
5.30pm (9.30pm in July and August).
☎ 01271 890407

Chapel Farm Gallery and Craft Centre

Cott Lane, Hobbs Hill
Croyde
Open: Easter to beginning of
November, daily 9am-5pm.
☎ 01271 890429

Continued over page

Village Museum

Bakehouse Centre, Caen Street
Braunton
Open: Easter-October, daily 10am-4pm; November-Easter daily except Sunday 10am-3pm. ☎ 01271 816688

Elliot Gallery

Hillsview
Braunton
Open: mid-April-October, daily 11am-5pm; November-December and March-mid-April, Thursday-Saturday 11am-4pm. ☎ 01271 812100

Ashford Gardens and Butterfly House

Ashford
Open: Whitsun to end of September, daily 9am-5pm.
☎ 01271 342880

Marwood Hill Gardens

Marwood
Open: All year, daily dawn-dusk. Plants sales daily 11am-5pm.
☎ 01271 342528

Barnstaple Heritage Centre

Queen Anne's Walk, The Strand
Barnstaple
Open: April-October, Monday-Saturday 10am-5pm; November-March, Monday-Friday 10am-4.30pm, Saturday 10am-3.30pm.
☎ 01271 373003

Museum of Barnstaple and North Devon

The Square
Barnstaple
Open: All year, Monday-Saturday 9.30am-5pm. Closed Christmas Day-New Years Day. ☎ 01271 346747

Brannam's Pottery

Roundswell Industrial Estate
Barnstaple
Open: All year, Monday-Friday 9am-5pm. Shop also open Saturday and Sunday (May-October).
☎ 01271 343035

North Devon Karting Centre

Pottington Business Park
Barnstaple
Open: April-June and September, Monday-Saturday 10.30am-5pm, Sunday 11am-5pm. July and August, Monday-Saturday 10am-6pm, Sunday 11am-5pm. October daily 11am-6pm. ☎ 01271 328460

Cobbaton Combat Collection

Chittlehampton, Umberleigh
Open: July and August daily 10am-5pm. April-June, September and mid-October, Sunday-Friday 10am-5pm.
☎ 01769 540740

North Devon Farm Park

Between Landkey and Swimbridge
Open: April-October daily 10am-5pm. Also limited opening in winter: ring for details. ☎ 01271 830255

Tordown Farm

Swimbridge
Open: Good Friday-September Saturday-Thursday 10am-5pm.
☎ 01271 830265

Broomhill Sculpture Garden and Art Gallery

Nr Barnstaple
Open: All year, Wednesday-Sunday 11am-4pm. July and August open Monday-Sunday. Closed 20 December-15 January.
☎ 01271 850262

Arlington Court (NT)

Arlington, near Barnstaple
Open: House, Garden and Park; April-October daily except Saturday, 11am-5pm (but also open on Bank Holiday Saturdays).
☎ 01271 850296

6. North-West Devon

Docton mill garden

South of Barnstaple a wide east-to-west rural corridor crosses North-West Devon. Only in the lower Torridge Valley have commerce, industry and tourism become established. Elsewhere Devon's northern delights are still often overlooked.

If the visitor first approaches this corner of the county from Barnstaple, as many will, along the busy bungalow-lined B3233 through Bickington, Fremington and Yelland, this backwoods character is not obvious. The new North Devon link road, the A39, connects Barnstaple with a high-level bridge downstream from Bideford.

INSTOW

Some 6 miles (9.5km) west of Barnstaple, **Instow** is reached, and can be swiftly bypassed if a distant destination beckons. But that would ignore a village of considerable distinction. Sited in a similar position on its estuary as Starcross is on the Exe in South Devon, Instow preserved its character by having the railway pass behind the sea front, and not in front as at Starcross. Also, it has splendid sands. Presumably a trick of the tides determines that some estuaries have muddy verges, and others have sandy beaches. Starcross is indisputably muddy, as indeed is Appledore, just across the Torridge from Instow. Mud is fine for wading birds and fishermen digging for worms, but not much fun for family beach parties.

The small seventeenth-century pier hints at an early history, but major events have passed Instow by. An 1838 promotion, advertising 'newly erected baths, replete with water, hot and cold, and shower bathing', seems to have come to nothing, for no trace remains of the baths. Not the least of Instow's charms is its position facing Appledore, to which a foot ferry plies in summer.

One site railway enthusiasts will want to visit is the award-winning signal box, a listed building that is complete with its original levers.

A mile south of Instow is **Tapeley Park**, an undistinguished house with a fine garden. Originally built in the eighteenth century, it was Gothicised in the 1880s, and finally altered in 1901. The Christie family own Tapeley – John Christie founded Glyndebourne in 1931 – and his daughter still lives here. The house is open to the public in the summer, and is worth seeing for the furniture.

Also close to Instow, the **Fremington Quay Heritage Centre** explores the history of this important 19th century port and pottery area.

BIDEFORD

Bideford is, by common consent, the most attractive town in the northern half of Devon, and is reached by an ancient bridge from East-the-Water. The bridge probably dates from the end of the fifteenth century when a previous wooden bridge was used as a framework for the stone structure. Because the timbers of the old bridge were of different lengths, the stone arches inherited this uneven characteristic. Several widenings and re-buildings later, the bridge at last failed in 1968, when two arches at the west end collapsed. During the months that elapsed before restoration was complete, all traffic had to travel round narrow lanes to the south, though a footbridge was strung across the gap for pedestrians. A high-level bypass road bridge, some distance downriver, was opened in 1987.

The eighteenth-century wars and the collapse of the Devon woollen industry killed off overseas commerce, leaving a coastal trade which has survived to this day. In the nineteenth century, Bideford was a transshipment port for goods going further up the Torridge. Cargoes were unloaded into barges, which continued upstream to Weare Gifford or, between 1836 and 1871, up the Rolle Canal from above Bideford to upstream from Great Torrington. Bideford is now once again the port of embarkation for Lundy.

Those who enjoyed the Instow Signal Box will want to visit the Bideford Railway heritage Centre which is run by the same group of enthusiasts. They hope to offer steam train rides by late 2004. Shopaholics should head for Atlantic Village which has outlets for named

The Grenville Family

Bideford's business through out history has been the sea and ship building, and the town owes much to the Grenville family, who first acquired land there in Norman times, an interest they retained until 1744. Trade with Sir Richard Grenville's colonies of Virginia and Carolina continued until their independence, and in the meantime a wool trade had developed with Spain, Holland and France. Bideford was involved at an early stage with Newfoundland.

brands at reduced prices as well as an adventure playground, maze, trampolines, a picnic area and café.

The town rises steeply from **the Quay**, and there are many corners worth seeking out. Bridgeland Street, at right angles to the Quay, is the street with most architectural pretensions. At the north end of the Quay is Charles Kingsley's statue. This nineteenth-century writer was born at Holne, on Dartmoor, and wrote at least some of his famous book *Westward Ho!* at the Royal Hotel in East-the-Water.

APPLEDORE AND WESTWARD HO!

Appledore must next be visited. Bideford and Appledore are inextricably linked and are only 10 minutes apart by car, though there is a pleasant 3 mile (5.5km) walk along the estuary edge footpath. The shipbuilding industry at Appledore is a present-day success story. The yard has moved with the times, is under

cover and turns out ships of considerable size. Furthermore, the yard has not spoiled the town. It is therefore appropriate that the **North Devon Maritime Museum** is sited here in Odun Road above the town. Models, tools and photographs tell the story of the area's long maritime tradition.

Appledore is in two parts: the southern part behind the Quay, and Irsha Street beyond the church. This is a long narrow street, just wide enough for a car, with tempting little cobbled courtyards and slipways. Halfway along are three waterside public houses, and, at the far end, a pleasant open space with views across to Bideford Bar, the treacherous sand-shifting channel through which ships have to make their way in and out of the estuary, and only negotiable for 3 hours around high water. Imagine running for the 'safety' of the Bar in the days of sail, in failing light, and on a falling tide!

Appledore Crafts is a co-operative gallery of 14 Devon craftsmen. Rather more hectic is Skern Lodge where both parents and children can enjoy activities from archery to climbing, kayaking to rafting.

Westward Ho!, the self-catering holiday resort just 'round the corner' from Appledore is probably the only place to take its name from a book and the only place I know to include an exclamation mark. A nineteenth-century development company used the interest evoked in Kingsley's book to create a watering place at the southern end of **Northam Burrows**, a 650-acre (260 hectares) stretch of sand dunes, salt marsh and pasture. A hotel, church, a few terraces and villas were built, followed by a golf course on the Burrows – even a promenade-type

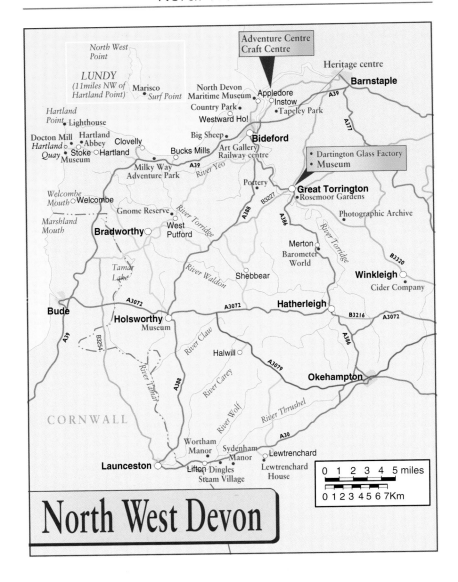

North West Point

LUNDY
(11miles NW of
Hartland Point)

Marisco
• Surf Point

Adventure Centre
Craft Centre

Heritage centre

Barnstaple

North Devon
Maritime Museum

Appledore
○Instow
• Tapeley Park

A39

A377

Hartland
Point • Lighthouse

Country Park •
Westward Ho!

Docton Mill   Hartland
Hartland ○ • Abbey   Clovelly
Quay • Stoke ○Hartland
Museum

Big Sheep •

Bideford

Art Gallery
Railway centre

• Dartington Glass Factory
• Museum

Bucks Mills ○

Milky Way
Adventure Park

A39

River Yeo

Pottery

Great Torrington
• Rosemoor Gardens

Welcombe
Mouth ○Welcombe

Gnome Reserve •

River Torridge

B3227

A388

A386

River Torridge

Photographic Archive

Marshland
Mouth

Bradworthy ○

West
Putford

Merton
Barometer
World

B3320

Tamar
Lake

River Waldon

Shebbear

Winkleigh ○
Cider Company

Bude

A3072

A3072

Hatherleigh

B3216

A3072

Holsworthy ○
Museum

River Claw

A386

A39

B3254

Halwill ○

A3079

Okehampton

River Tamar

A388

River Carey

River Wolf

River Thrushel

CORNWALL

A30

Wortham
Manor

Sydenham
Manor ○Lewtrenchard

Launceston ○

Lifton Dingles
Steam Village

Lewtrenchard
House

| 0 | 1 | 2 | 3 | 4 | 5 miles |

0 1 2 3 4 5 6 7Km

North West Devon

pier, but the waves demolished it very quickly. Kipling was educated here in the United Services College, and later wrote up his schoolboy experiences in *Stalky & Co.* Last century, Westward Ho! expanded as a chalet, caravan and camping resort. The beach, of course, is wonderful; 2 miles (3km) of golden sand, backed by the Pebble Ridge which protects the Burrows from the Atlantic breakers, though now and again it has to be repaired. Northam Burrows is now a Country Park, administered by Devon County Council, and an excellent twenty-page

Above: Instow

Below: Bideford Bridge

guidebook describes every aspect of life on the Burrows, where the pursuits of riding and golf can be carried out, and explains where bathing is dangerous and where it is safe.

South-westwards from Westward Ho! the cliffs rise gradually and curve in a parabola towards Bucks Mills. But North-West Devon extends many miles to the south, and this vast inland district should be described before ending at the Cornish border.

GREAT TORRINGTON

Great Torrington is a hilltop town, the more attractive parts of which motorists normally miss. A long street of dull buildings ensures that the casual passer-by goes on his way oblivious of its charms. Visitors are strongly advised to penetrate to the heart of the town and explore for themselves. From one of the car parks on Castle Hill the land falls away down a steep slope of bracken and gorse. Round three sides of Great Torrington is an open common. Indeed, Great Torrington is sometimes spoken of as being the English Jerusalem by those who have visited the Holy Land. The slopes are contoured by many well kept paths, and a walk round the circuit probably takes 1 hour. The town is focused on the Square, where the Town Hall stands, with the Market House at the bottom end. The museum is in the Town Hall as is Torrington 1646 heritage centre recreating an experience of life in the seventeenth century. Round the corner in Fore Street is the Plough Theatre, Cinema and Arts Centre, a lively community entertainments complex where something is going on most days.

Great Torrington has several thriving industries including the Dartington Glass factory, which opens its doors to visitors and glass is also on sale.

During the Civil War, in 1646, the church, which had been used as a powder magazine, was crowded with Royalist prisoners when the powder exploded, killing several hundred men. A mound in the churchyard may be the mass grave.

Just south of Great Torrington, beside the A3124, are the Rosemoor Gardens, well worth visiting for the variety of shrubs and plants growing in this sheltered valley.

North of Great Torrington, at Monkeigh, the pottery is worth a visit, as is the photographic archive at Beaford to the east. Here there are thousands of images of 19th century rural Devon in a fine old house, which is also used for community projects.

The A386 going south towards Hatherleigh soon reaches Merton where Barometer World is a museum of the history of barometers in a workshop where barometers are still crafted. The A386 now continues through the ball clay area round Meeth and Petrockstowe. This deposit matches up geologically with the ball clay beds in the Bovey basin in South Devon.

NORTH OF DARTMOOR

Hatherleigh is a small market town with an old public house, the George, worth driving many miles to see. Market day is a wonderful gathering of rubicund farmers.

East of Hatherleigh, at Winkleigh, at the Cider Company, visitors can learn about the traditional craft of cider making as well as testing the product. There is also a small craft centre.

South of Hatherleigh, bestriding the A30 west of Okehampton, are three country houses of more than usual interest. The first is **Lewtrenchard House** near **Lewtrenchard** village. This seventeenth-century house, now a hotel, was much altered by its famous nineteenth-century occupant, the Rev Sabine Baring-Gould (1834-1924), the author, folk song collector, antiquarian, and hymn writer (the author of 'Onward, Christian Soldiers').

The second house, **Sydenham Manor**, about 4 miles (6km) away along narrow lanes, is perhaps the finest Jacobean house in the county, but not open to the public.

About 7 or 8 miles (11-13km) north-west of Sydenham, beyond the A30 and **Lifton**, is **Wortham Manor**, an even earlier house, of the late fifteenth or early sixteenth century, somewhat reconstructed inside in the seventeenth. This splendid stone house was deteriorating when the Landmark Trust purchased it in 1969, and it has been converted into three holiday flats. The project received a Civic Trust Award in 1975. Despite being apparently at the back-of-beyond, this house has the new A30 passing nearby.

A very large reservoir to serve North Devon and Plymouth at Roadford on the River Wolf, just 4 miles (6km) to the north-east, offers fishing, sailing and picnic opportunities. Also close to Lifton, at Milford, is **Dingle's Steam Village**, which explores the history of steam power in the country, with various traction and other engines. There is also a village store selling souvenirs, and a childrens' play area.

The part of Devon around **Halwill** has a number of large Forestry Commission plantations, and several walks through the trees are laid out. As forestry operations can alter these arrangements, visitors are advised to contact the Forestry Commission office at Cookworthy Moor, near Beaworthy.

Holsworthy

Holsworthy is a market town serving a wide area of rural Devon, and is best visited on Wednesdays, when the Square swarms with traders and shoppers. Once a year, in July, the ancient St Peter's Fair is held in the town – as it has been since 1185! – and one of the charming traditions is the Pretty Maid Ceremony. This began in 1841 when a sum of money was left so that a local single woman under thirty, noted for her looks, quietness and attendance at church, should be given a small financial award. A seventeenth-century manor house contains the town museum.

At **West Putford**, not far from Bradworthy, is the **Gnome Reserve and Wildflower Garden**, where, in a woodland setting, over 1,000 gnomes may be seen living their immobile lives in a 'natural' environment. **Bradworthy** is an interesting village built round an enormous open space once used as a market. The well stocked shops are worth seeking out.

Not far away, and literally on the border with Cornwall, are the **Tamar Lakes,** two reservoirs straddling the infant River Tamar, the county boundary. In a part of Devon where there are few stretches of water, the lakes are much frequented by waterfowl and ornithologists. Sailing and boardsailing are possible, and there is a picnic area and water's edge footpaths. The upper lake is stocked with trout and the lower lake is a coarse fishery.

To the west of Bideford the A39 heads towards Clovelly, soon passing the **Big Sheep,** a farm experience. Children can touch the animals or try the adventure playground. Beyond, **Bucks Mills** is soon reached. The village has many similarities with Clovelly, our next stop; a steep, cottage-lined road, in a valley leading to a final drop to the beach. Bucks Mills is small and has a free car park at the top of the village. At the bottom a massive lime kiln is built above the beach.

From here the white buildings of Clovelly can be seen spilling out through the woods like a frozen coastal waterfall, and is best reached by the Hobby Drive (open from Easter to October for a small charge). This leaves the A39 a mile (1.5km) west of Bucks Cross and follows the contours of the wooded slopes for 3 miles (5km) to Clovelly. The name Hobby was given to it as its construction was the hobby of Sir James Hamlyn Williams, the landowner in the nineteenth century. Close to Bucks Mills, the **Milky Way Adventure Park** is the largest indoor children's adventure park in the south-west, with all the usual entertainments plus a few novelties – laser rifles and commando-type nets and swings.

CLOVELLY AND HARTLAND

Clovelly is the ace in the North-West Devon pack. There is nothing else like it in Great Britain. A very steep cobbled street lined with attractive flower-bedecked cottages occupies the entire width of a narrow north-facing valley. All cars are kept at the top, and supplies for properties in

Hartland Point

However one returns, on foot or in a car, **Hartland Point** must be visited. This is Devon's own Land's End, a 90-degree turning point on the coast of the West Country, and here the scenery changes dramatically. Left behind are the gentle slopes and wooded combes of the Bristol Channel, for the cliffs and shoreline take on a malignant savagery not often seen even on an Atlantic-facing coast. Fretted reefs of black rock reach out like teeth on a saw.

There is a large car park (small fee), but no beach. Strongly recommended is a short stroll onto the west-facing coast, not visible from the car park. Walk along the coast path beside a wall outside the Trinity House gate as far as the first stile, from where the lighthouse can be seen. Beyond looms Lundy, 11 miles (17.5km) away, and this is the nearest point to it on the mainland.

Hartland Quay

If Clovelly is the ace in the pack, **Hartland Quay** is the trump! On a calm day in summer everything appears benign. But a struggle to the Quay in a force nine gale in January is a very different matter. Enormous waves crash on this harsh and uncompromising coast. Yet, for over 250 years, a small harbour served this remote corner of Devon and gave a name to the spot. Skilfully sailed small boats edged in through the reefs, bringing coal, lime, slate, planks, nails and numerous domestic supplies. The record of the arrival of lead for the church roof is still in existence.

The last ship to discharge cargo was the *Rosamond Jane* in 1893, and by then the harbour had already begun to break up under the relentless battering of the Atlantic. By the 1920s it had all gone, and a major effort of the imagination is required to see where it stood. An excellent, well-illustrated 48-page book *Hartland Quay: The Story of a Vanished Port* is obtainable from the **Hartland Quay Museum**, giving the full history of this fascinating place. Two small rows of buildings at the Quay face the 'Street', where there is a hotel with a bar, a shop and lavatories. On the cliff to the north is a ruin which as it stands is probably an eighteenth-century folly, but may have been built from a earlier lookout.

North Devon Cliffs near Hartland

the valley have to be carried down or manhandled on sledges. The donkeys, which once provided trans-

port, are retired, and there is a back road Land Rover service to the Red Lion on the Quay which takes

Tarka the Otter and the Tarka Trail

Henry Williamson settled in Georgeham, a village inland from Croyde, after his return from the 1914-18 War. There he wrote a book dealing with the life and death of an otter among the otter hunts in the Land of the Two Rivers, as the country between the Taw and the Torridge is known. The book – *Tarka the Otter* – was published in 1928 and won the Hawthornden Prize. Though Williamson lived to the north of the Torridge it was that river that he loved and he had his animal-hero born in a holt near the canal bridge on the river between Weare Gifford and Landcross, two hamlets about 3 km (2 miles) apart, Weare Gifford being about 5 km (3 miles) downriver from Great Torrington. At the end of the book the waters of Torridge close over the heads of Tarka and Deadlock, the otter-hound, as they fight their last battle close to Landcross.

Tarka the Otter is a book which arouses differing emotions: is it an indictment of the hunting of a beautiful creature by a man appalled by the casual slaughter of the trenches, or a glorification of country values, including otter-hunting?

Williamson wrote further books, several of which also document animal lives – *Salar the Salmon, Chakchek the Peregrine* – each of which, and most especially *The Lone Swallows*, evoke the atmosphere of North Devon in the first half of this century. He briefly moved to Norfolk, but when he died in 1977 he was buried at Georgeham.

An interesting project that takes its name from Williamson's otter hero has set up headquarters in Great Torrington – in the Eric Palmer Community Centre – with the aim of promoting conservation as well as recreation and tourism in North Devon. One aspect of the Tarka Project is of interest to walkers, as it involves the waymarking of the Tarka Trail, a 180 mile (290 km) walk. The walk is a figure-of-eight based on Barnstaple, going east and then north to Lynton and returning via Ilfracombe, and south through Bideford and Great Torrington to Okehampton, returning on a route to the east.

people back up the hill. A beneficent landowner ensures that the place remains unspoilt, and despite the many thousands of visitors it receives annually, Clovelly has the strength of character to rise above the tourists. The tiny quayside has a period air about it. Fishermen are busy with their tackle and a lifeboat is stationed there.

The 8 mile (13km) walk along the **North Devon Coast Path** to **Hartland Point** is highly recommended, particularly in spring when the bluebells and primroses are in bloom. As there is no public transport at the far end, however, one must either backtrack or arrange to be met by car. The first part, as far as **Mouth Mill**, is in the Clovelly estate, and passes various small summerhouse follies, such as Angels' Wings, and Miss Woodall's Seat, an incredible clifftop viewpoint. The path descends to sea level at Mouth Mill, and there is another valley a short distance further on at Windbury but, having passed these, the path stays high all the way to Hartland Point. Just before the Point is reached, a truly beautiful beach will be seen,

Shipload Bay, a rarity in these parts – a sandy beach, at least at low tide. The National Trust recently rebuilt the path down to the beach as the previous one had been swept away in a landslide.

The 3 mile (5km) clifftop walk from the Point to Hartland Quay is another fine walk, and is short enough for a there-and-back ramble. But most people will arrive at **Hartland Quay** by road.

The museum has relics from centuries of shipwrecks on this notorious stretch of coast as well as on local history and smuggling.

In the days when England had an intensive railway network, **Hartland** boasted it was further from a railway than anywhere else in the country. Cars have made a difference, of course, but it is still remote, and the inhabitants are more than usually self-reliant. The architecture is not outstanding, but the main street has charm, and to enter the shops or public houses is to experience old-fashioned service and courtesy. Inland from Hartland Town are extensive commercial tree plantations.

Hartland's great treasure, apart from the coastline, is its parish church at **Stoke**, 1 mile (1.5km) back from the sea, and over 2 miles (3km) from Hartland Town. The tower combines strength with grace. Inside, the main features are the late fifteenth-century rood screen, bench ends and wagon roofs. The church is worth cycling 30 miles (48km) against the wind to see, not only for the building but for its setting in a wind-torn landscape. Trees bow before the westerlies, gravestones lean, and there is a timeless aspect about everything which makes a mere mortal feel uplifted by the permanence of the place.

Hartland Abbey, a family home since 1539 with its furniture, porcelain and other family collections, is nearby. The Abbey was built in 1157 and dissolved by Henry VIII who then gifted it to the Seargeant of his Wine Cellar. Today visitors can also enjoy a beautiful woodland walk to the beach or wander the gardens, part of which was designed by Gertrude Jekyll.

A walk of about a mile (1.5km) southwards leads to **Speke's Mill Mouth** and the finest waterfall on the north-west Devon coast – a sheer 54ft (19m) drop. This walk is well worth doing, passing on the way the sliced-off hill known as St Catherine's Tor. Speke's Mill Mouth is the second valley going south. In Speke's Valley, **Docton Mill** is a working mill with Saxon origins set in delightful grounds. Its garden is open to the public, either side of the mill leat.

There is one further place on the coast that drivers can visit – **Welcombe Mouth**, though the lanes are narrow and there is little provision for parking. The church is a couple of miles inland. A sandy beach is exposed at low tide and the place is unspoilt, except for the cars. To escape one can climb out of Welcombe Mouth up the coast path to the south and as steeply descend to **Marsland Mouth**, a kind of replica valley, but devoid of vehicular intrusion, and briefly pretend that the twenty-first century doesn't exist, for Marsland Mouth is untainted by technology. What is more, it is only half Devon; beyond the stream is Cornwall, but that's another story…

In and around Bideford & Appledore

Tapeley Park

Instow
Open: Easter to October, Sunday-Friday, 10am-5pm.
☎ (01271) 342371

Fremington Quay Heritage Centre

Fremington
Open: All year, Tuesday-Sunday, 10am-5pm (10pm from April-September).
☎ 01271 378783

Instow Signal Box

Instow
Open: Easter-October, Sunday & Bank Holidays, 2-5pm.
☎ 01237 425072

Bideford Railway Heritage Centre

Bideford
Open: Easter-October, Sunday & Bank Holidays, 2-5pm. Also open weekdays if volunteers are available.
☎ 01237 429072

Atlantic Village

Off the A39, Clovelly road, west of Bideford
Open: All year, Monday-Saturday, 10am-6pm (8pm on Thursday), Sunday, 10.30am-430pm.
☎ 01237 422544

Appledore Crafts

5 Bude Street, Appledore
Open: April-October, daily 10am-6pm, October-December, Wednesday-Sunday, 10am-4pm, January-March, Saturday & Sunday, 10am-4pm.
☎ 01237 423547

Skern Lodge Adventure Days

Appledare
Open: All year for groups, School Holidays for individuals.
☎ 01237 475992

North Devon Maritime Museum

Odum House,
Appledore.
Open: Easter to October, daily 2-5pm (also open May-September, Monday-Friday, 11am-1pm.
☎ (01237) 422064

Burton Art Gallery & Museum

Kingsley Road, Bideford
Open all year Tuesday-Saturday, 10am-4pm, Sunday, 2-4pm (open to 5pm Easter-October).
☎ (01237) 471455

Northam Burrows Country Park

Open at any resonable time.

Away from the Coast in North-West Devon

Dartington Glass Factory

Great Torrington
Open: All year. Factory Tour/Visitor Centre – 9.30am-5pm Monday to Friday. Factory Shop – 9.30am-5pm Monday to Friday, Saturday, 10-5pm and Sunday, 10-4pm.
☎ (01805) 626242

Great Torrington Museum and 1646

Open: March-September, Monday-Saturday 10.30am-5pm. October-February, Monday-Friday 11am-4.30pm.
Sunday 11am-1pm.
☎ (01805) 624324 and 626146

Rosemoor Gardens

Great Torrington
Open: 10am-5pm (6pm in summer) daily, all year.
☎ (01805) 624067

Monkleigh Pottery

Monkleigh
Open: February-December, daily 10am-6pm
☎ 01805 623194

Photographic Archive

Greenwarren House
Beaford
Open: Telephone for details
☎ 01805 603201

Winkleigh Cider Company

Western Barn, Hatherleigh Road, Winkleigh
Open: All year, Monday-Saturday, 9am-5pm.
☎ 01837 83560

Barometer World

Merton
Open: 9am-5pm Tuesday to Saturday, all year.
☎ (01805) 603443

Holsworthy Museum Manor Offices

Open February-December, Monday, Tuesday, Thursday, Friday, 11am-1pm. Wednesday, 11am-3.30pm.
☎ (01409) 259337

Dingles Steam Village

Open: 10.30am-5.30pm Saturday to Thursday, Easter to the end of October.
☎ (01566) 783425

Gnome Reserve and Wildflower Garden

West Putford
Open: 10am-6pm daily, mid March to end of October.
☎ (0870) 8459012

Big Sheep

Abbotsham, Bideford
Open: 10am-6pm daily, Easter to October. 10am-5pm weekend and half-terms only, November to March.
☎ (01237) 472366

The North-West Devon Coast

Milky Way Adventure Park

Open: Easter-October, daily 10.30am-6pm. Also open weekends and school holidays in winter, 11am-5pm.
☎ (01237) 431255

Hartland Abbey

House & Gardens: April-October, Wednesday, Thursday, Sunday & bank Holidays, 2-5.30pm and Tuesdays in July & August. Gardens also open Tuesday & Wednesday.
☎ (01237) 441264/441234

Hartland Quay Museum

Open: One week at Easter and late – May-early October, daily 11am-5pm.

Docton Mill and Gardens

South of Hartland Point
Open: March-October, daily 10am-6pm. November-March, by appointment.
☎ (01237) 441369

ACCOMMODATION

There is a very wide range of accommodation available throughout the area, from hotels, guest-houses, farmhouses, bed and breakfast establishments, inns and youth hostels to caravan and camp sites, self-catering in all types of properties – visitors can even stay in a lighthouse on Lundy Island – and camping barns.

All forms of accommodation within the Exmoor National Park and the nearby coast are covered in the 'Exmoor Visitor' and 'Exmoor Coast and Country' each of which is produced annually and available from National Park Visitor Centres. These are listed towards the end of this Fact File.

Hotels, Guest-Houses, Bed and Breakfast, Inns

Details of this type of accommodation can be obtained from the local Tourist Information Offices. These are listed towards the end of this Fact File.

Farm Holidays

Exmoor Holiday Group
(Farm Holidays)
☎ 01398 323278

Hostels

Details of YHA hostels in the area are available from:
Youth Hostel Association
Via Gellia Mill
Bonsall
Matlock
Derbyshire
☎ 01629 824724

Self—Catering, Caravan and Camping Sites

Any of the Tourist Information Centres listed later in the Fact File will supply brochures giving up-to-date details.

Exmoor for the Disabled

Under the Exmoor *Access for All* Scheme people with a range of disabilities are able to enjoy greater access to the National Park. The range of options is being increased constantly and already includes a boardwalk near Robber's Bridge, trails near Selworthy Beacon and Webber's Post and pondside access at Pile's Mill.

A leaflet – Access for All – gives details of the trails at Robber's Bridge and Webber's Post, and one at Bossington.

A guide to all facilities – *Accessible Exmoor* – is available from National Park Visitor Centres.

The following associations offer specialist information:

Fact File

Riding for the Disabled Association
☎ 01752 894348

Somerset County Association for the Blind
☎ 01823 333818

Devon County Association for the Blind
☎ 01392 876666

CRAFTS

In addition to the craft centres mentioned in the text there are many others. Two leaflets, one by the Exmoor Producers Association and the other titled North Devon Art and Craft Trail are available from Tourist Information Centres and list some of the better sites.

FOOD

Recommending restaurants is fraught with danger. Much safer is to recommend the publication *Taste of the West*, published by areas within the West Country which lists not only good places to eat, but places where food, including local specialities, can be purchased. It is available from Tourist Information Offices.

PUBLIC TRANSPORT

Having a low population density, Exmoor and North Devon suffer from a lack of public transport. However, to make the most of what is available ask for the leaflets on public transport at the local Tourist Information Centres. Of particular interest to walkers on the moor who wish to use public transport to support linear walks will be the Exmoor and West Somerset Public Transport Guide prepared jointly by Devon CC, Somerset CC and the Exmoor National Park Authority. This is available from National Park Offices. The Guide contains details of one-day, three-day and one-week passes.

RECREATION

Climbing

Baggy Point is one of the major climbing areas of the West Country with routes suitable for both beginners and experts. The area is covered by *Baggy – Sun, Sea and Slabs, A Climber's Guide* published by Void Publishing.

Lundy Island is also popular with climbers. It is covered by the Climbers Club guide *Lundy*.

Please note that restrictions apply to certain Lundy cliffs during seabird nesting.

Fact File

Cycling

Though it is an upland area, the roads across Exmoor offer excellent opportunities for the cyclist, though the number wishing to pit their strength against Porlock or Countisbury hills is likely to remain small. For off–road enthusiasts there are limited possibilities, though trails have been created near Wimbleball Lake and also on the northern flank of the Brendon Hills. The Exmoor National Park Authority has prepared a Code of Conduct for off–road cyclists in the Park. This is available from all Park Information Offices.

The major trails for cyclists in the area lie in Devon. The Devon Coast to Coast Trail (National Cycle Network Route No. 27) links Ilfracombe and Plymouth via Braunton and Barnstaple. The West Country Way (NCN 3) links Bristol to Padstow, the section within the area covered by this book running westwards into Barnstaple having linked Taunton, Tiverton and Bampton. The route then links Barnstaple with Bideford, Great Torrington and Holsworthy before reaching Bude in Cornwall. Finally, the Tarka Trail (also a walker's path – see below) follows a disued railway south from Ilfracombe. Not surprisingly, cycle hire has increased as a result of these trails. There are many opportunities, but worth considering are:

Tarka Trail Cycle Hire
The Railway Station
Barnstaple
☎ 01271 324202

Bideford Bicycle Hire
Torrington Street
East the Water
Bideford
Tel: 01237 424123

Closer to the National Park, try:

Biketrail
01598 763263/763496

Biketrail
Fremington Quay
Nr Barnstaple
Tel: 01231 372586/378783

Guided mountain bike tours are available from:

Toms Tours
Broadwood Farm, Dunster
☎ 01643 821953

Fishing

The sea fishing is excellent from most of the ports, villages and towns of the Somerset and Devon coasts and some places offer fishing from boats. Fishing is also possible at Wimbleball Reservoir and several other lakes. For details contact:

Those interested in learning the gentle art of fly fishing in beautiful surroundings can contact:

South West Lakes Trust
Higher Coombepark
Lewdon

Nr Okehampton
Devon EX20 4QT
☎ 01837 871565

Hart Flyfishing
Tel: 01643 831101 or 07971 198559

Golf

There are golf courses at:

Barnstaple
01271 378378

Great Torrington
01805 622229

Ilfracombe
Hele Bay
☎ 01271 862176/862050

Ilfracombe and Woolacombe Golf Range
Woolacombe
☎ 01271 866222

Minehead
☎ 01643 702057

Mortehoe
☎ 01271 870566

Barnstaple
☎ 01271 378378

Saunton
☎ 01271 812436

Westward Ho!
☎ 01237 473817

Woolacombe
☎ 01237 870173

Leisure Centres

North Devon Leisure Centre
Seven Brethren Bank
Barnstaple
☎ 01271 373361

West Somerset Sports and Leisure Centre
Bircham Road
Alcombe
☎ 01643 708815

Riding

Exmoor and North Devon are ideal for riding and have many places where horses can be hired. For up-to-date information contact any TIC.
Visitors intending to bring their own horses could contact:

Exmoor Stabling Group
c/o Twitchen Farm
Challacombe
☎ 01598 763568

Swimming Pools

Aquasplash
Seaward Road
Minehead
☎ 01643 708000

Cascades
Croyde Bay
01271 890884

Ilfracombe Swimming Pool
Hillsborough Road
☎ 01271 864480

Knights Templar First School
Liddymore Road
Watchet
☎ 01984 633429

Fact File

Walking

The area covered by this book is great walking country. Exmoor is marvellous for walkers, with an interesting range of scenery and magnificent views. North Devon, particularly the coast, is also excellent for the walker. The area is traversed by three long–distance footpaths:

The South-West Coast Path — is Britain's longest National Trail. The Path is waymarked by the acorn symbol of National Trails.
The Two Moors Way — is a Recreational Path, that is a long-distance path which is not a National Trail, but one that is waymarked and maintained throughout. The Way runs from Ivybridge to Lynmouth, crossing the eastern edge of Dartmoor and central Exmoor. On Exmoor the Way heads north across the Park to Withypool, then bears west, passing south of Simonsbath before turning north to reach Lynmouth.

The Tarka Trail — is another Recreational Path forming a figure-of-eight centred on Barnstaple. The northern circle heads east from Barnstaple to Brayford, then crosses western Exmoor to Lynton (for part of this route the Trail is coincident with the Two Moors Way). From Lynton the Trail follows the coastal National Trail back to Barnstaple.

There are many guide books to walks on Exmoor, but walkers who do not want to bother with guide book, map and compass can join one of the guided walks offered by the National Park Authority. The *Exmoor Visitor*, available from all National Park Visitor Centres has dates and details of these walks.
It is also possible to make a holiday of walking the moor. Visitors interested in such holidays can contact:

West Country Walks
c/o Harwill House
Victoria Street
Combe Martin
☎ 01271 883487

Moorland Rover
Corner Cottage
Silver Street
Bampton
☎ 01398 332372

TRANSPORT

By Car
The most straightforward approach is from Junction 23 of the M5 then through Bridgwater and along the A39, which goes north of the Quantocks to reach Williton and Exmoor. Junction 27 allows the A361 to be followed to Barnstaple and north Devon.

By Rail
The West Somerset Railway links Minehead to Bishops Lydeard near Taunton. Barnstaple has a main line (Wales and West) station. Trains run from here along the 'Tarka Line' that follows the Taw valley to Exeter.

By Coach
There are long–distance coaches from major cities to Taunton and Barnstaple via Bristol and Exeter.

By Air
There are regional airports at Bristol and Exeter.

TOURIST INFORMATION CENTRES

National Park Visitor Centres

Seacot
13 Cross Street
Combe Martin
☎ 01271 883319

County Gate
A39 **Countisbury**
☎ 01598 741321

Fore Street
Dulverton
☎ 01398 323841

Dunster Steep
Dunster
☎ 01643 821835

The Esplanade
Lynmouth
☎ 01598 752509

Written enquiries should be made to:
Exmoor National Park Authority
Exmoor House
Dulverton
Somerset
TA22 9HL
☎ 01398 323665
Fax: 01398 323150

Other Information Centres

North Devon Museum
The Square
Barnstaple
☎ 01271 375000

Caen Street car park
Braunton
☎ 01271 816400

The Quay, Kingsley Road
Bideford
☎ 01271 816400

The Square
Holsworthy
☎ 01409 254185

Landmark, The Seafront
Ilfracombe
☎ 01271 863001

Town Hall, Lee Road
Lynton
☎ 01598 752225

17 Friday Street
Minehead
☎ 01643 702624

West End, High Street
Porlock
☎ 01643 863150

South Street Car Park
Great Torrington
☎ 01805 626140

The Esplanade
Woolacombe
☎ 01271 870553

Fact File

INTERNET WEB SITES

Exmoor Tourist Association www.exmoortourism.tv
Exmoor National Park www.exmoor-nationalpark.gov.uk
Devon Tourism www.devon-cc.gov.uk/tourism
North Devon Tourism www.northdevon.co.uk
Somerset Tourism www.somerset.gov.uk/tourism/default.htm

USEFUL ADDRESSES

**Exmoor National Park
Authority**
Exmoor House
Dulverton
Somerset
TA22 9HL
☎ 01398 323665
Fax: 01398 323150

South West Tourism
Woodwater Park
Exeter
EX2 5WT
☎ 0870 442 0830

Devon Tourism
Devon County Council
County Hall
Exeter
Devon EX2 4QQ
☎ 01392 382284

Somerset Tourism
Somerset Visitor Centre
Sedgemoor Services
M5 Motorway (South)
Axbridge BS26 2UF
☎ 01934 750833

WEATHER

A weather forecast for Exmoor and North Devon (and the remainder of the South-West Peninsula) is available by ringing 0891 141203. The forecast covers the next 48-72 hours and is updated daily at 7am and 7pm.

Index

Index

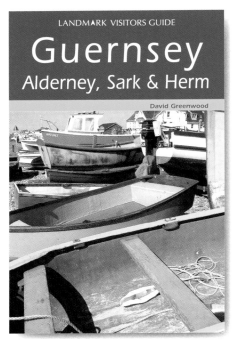
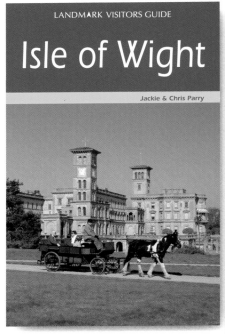

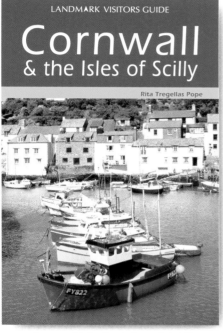
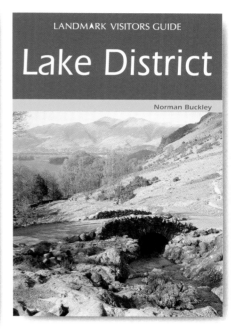
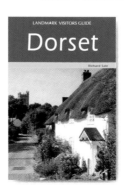

Notes

ARRIVE INFORMED WITH YOUR
LANDMARK VISITORS GUIDE

Visit: www.landmarkpublishing.co.uk

• Algarve	1-901522-92-X	£6.50
• Antigua & Barbuda (2nd Edition)	1-84306-061-2	£7.50
• Aruba, Bonaire & Curaçao	1-901522-04-0	£7.95
• Bahamas	1-901522-00-8	£7.95
• Barbados	1-901522-32-6	£6.95
• Bermuda	1-901522-07-5	£7.95
• Bruges (5th Edition)	1-84306-119-8	£5.95
• Cayman Islands	1-84306-037-X	£6.95
• Cornwall & The Isles of Scilly (7th Edition)	1-84306-123-6	£10.95
• Côte d'Azur	1-901522-29-6	£6.50
• Cracow (2nd edition)	1-84306-033-7	£7.95
• Devon (2nd Edition)	1-84306-003-5	£10.95
• Dordogne	1-901522-67-9	£9.95
• Dorset (3rd Edition)	1-84306-116-3	£10.95
• East Anglia	1-901522-58-X	£5.00
• Exmoor & North Devon (2nd Edition)	1-901522-95-4	£5.95
• Florida: The Gulf Coast (2nd Edition)	1-84306-059-0	£7.95
• Florida: The Keys (2nd Edition)	1-84306-040-X	£7.95
• France from the Channel Ports	1-84306-054-X	£9.95
• Gambia, the (2nd edition)	1-84306-077-9	£7.95
• Gran Canaria	1-901522-19-9	£6.50
• Guernsey, Alderney & Sark (2nd Edition)	1-84306-076-0	£10.95
• Hereford	1-901522-72-5	£5.95
• Iceland (2nd Edition)	1-84306-038-8	£12.95
• India: Goa	1-901522-23-7	£7.95
• Isle of Wight (3rd Edition)	1-84306-120-1	£7.50
• Italian Lakes (6th edition)	1-84306-035-3	£11.95
• Jamaica	1-901522-31-8	£6.95
• Jersey (6th edition)	1-84306-090-6	£10.95
• Kefalonia (2nd Edition)	1-84306-122-8	£7.50
• Lake District (3rd Edition)	1-84306-119-X	£9.95
• Languedoc	1-901522-79-2	£7.95
• Lesvos	1-84306-118-X	£7.95

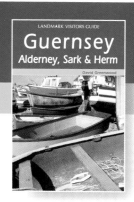
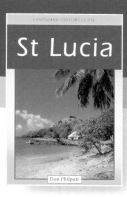
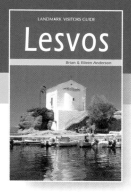

UK   World   Europe

- Madeira   1-901522-50-4   £8.95
- **Mull, Iona & Staffa**   1-84306-078-7   £6.50
- New Forest (2nd Edition)   1-84306-062-0   £6.50
- **Northern Cyprus (2nd Edition)**   1-84306-056-6   £9.95
- North Wales & Snowdonia   1-84306-043-4   £9.95
- **Oxford**   1-84306-022-1   £6.50
- Peak District (2nd edition)   1-84306-097-3   £9.95
- **Puerto Rico**   1-901522-34-2   £7.95
- Rhodes   1-84306-121-X   £10.95
- **Riga & its beaches, Latvia (2nd edition)**   1-84306-096-5   £9.95
- Scotland   1-901522-18-0   £5.00
- **Shakespeare Country & the Cotswolds (2nd Ed)**   1-84306-002-7   £10.95
- Somerset   1-901522-40-7   £9.95
- **Sri Lanka**   1-901522-37-7   £5.00
- St Lucia (4th Editon)   1-84306-099-X   £6.95
- **Tenerife**   1-901522-17-2   £6.50
- The National Forest   1-84306-106-6   £5.95
- **Ticino**   1-901522-74-1   £8.95
- Trinidad & Tobago (2nd Edition)   1-84306-115-5   £6.50
- **Vendée**   1-901522-76-8   £7.95
- Virgin Islands, US & British (2nd Editon)   1-84306-036-1   £11.95
- **Yorkshire Dales & Moors**   1-901522-41-5   £10.95
- Zakinthos (2nd Edition)   1-84306-024-8   £7.50

Prices subject to change

Landmark Publishing Ltd
Ashbourne Hall, Cokayne Ave, Ashbourne, Derbyshire, DE6 1EJ England
Tel 01335 347349   Fax 01335 347303   e-mail landmark@clara.net

Published by:
Landmark Publishing Ltd,
Ashbourne Hall, Cokayne Avenue, Ashbourne, Derbyshire DE6 1EJ England
E-mail landmark@clara.net Web-site www.landmarkpublishing.co.uk

ISBN 1-84306-142-2

British Library Cataloguing in Publication Data:
A catalogue record for this book is available from the British Library

Print: Gutenberg Press Ltd, Malta
Cartography: Mark Titterton
Design: James Allsopp

Front cover: Arlington Court
Back Cover top: Tarr Steps
Back Cover bottom: Rhenish tower, Lynmouth